# Ceramics
## of the '20s & '30s

A Collector's Guide

D1509053

# Ceramics
## of the '20s & '30s

### A Collector's Guide

Frankie Leibe

Special Consultants:
Beverley Adams and Beth Adams

**MILLER'S CERAMICS OF THE '20s & '30s: A COLLECTOR'S GUIDE**
by Frankie Leibe
Special consultants: Beverley Adams and Beth Adams

First published in Great Britain in 1999 by Miller's, a division of
Mitchell Beazley, imprints of Octopus Publishing Group Ltd,
Michelin House, 81 Fulham Road, London SW3 6RB

Miller's is a registered trademark of Octopus Publishing Group Ltd

Copyright © Octopus Publishing Group Ltd 1999

Executive Editor **Alison Starling**
Executive Art Editor **Vivienne Brar**
Senior Editor **Anthea Snow**
Assistant Editor **Clare Peel**
Designers **Louise Griffiths & Adrian Morris**
Indexer **Sue Farr**
Production **Rachel Staveley**

Specially commissioned photography by **Tim Ridley**
Jacket photograph by **Steve Tanner**

All rights reserved. No part of this work may be reproduced or utilized in
any form or by any means, electronic or mechanical, including photocopying,
recording or by any information storage and retrieval system, without the
prior written permission of the publisher.

The publishers will be grateful for any information that will assist them in
keeping future editions up to date. Although all reasonable care has been
taken in the preparation of this book, neither the publishers nor the compilers
can accept any liability for any consequence arising from the use thereof,
or the information contained therein.

ISBN 1 84000 068 6

A CIP catalogue record for this book is available from the British Library

Set in Bembo, Frutiger and Shannon
Colour reproduction by Vimnice Printing Press Co. Ltd., Hong Kong
Produced by Toppan Printing Co., (HK) Ltd.
Printed and bound in China

Jacket (left to right): sugar-shaker by Crown Ducal, vase by Clarice Cliff, sugar-
bowl by Susie Cooper, vase by Keith Murray, and cup and saucer by Paragon

# contents

# Where to start

The qualities that made Art Deco ceramics popular in the 1920s and 1930s – **bright colours, bold new forms, exuberant patterns**, and a **wide range of styles** and **prices** – are those that make Art Deco such a popular field of collecting today. The Exposition des Arts Décoratifs et Industriels Modernes ("Exhibition of Decorative and Modern Industrial Arts") held in Paris in 1925 was both the showcase for the new style and the inspiration for its name. World War II cut short the production of Art Deco ceramics, and it was not until the late 1960s and early 1970s that a few perceptive collectors began to buy pieces by makers who are now internationally recognized, such as Clarice Cliff, at prices that make today's buyers green with envy.

Production of Art Deco ceramics was prolific – there were over 400 factories in the Staffordshire area alone – and novice collectors should spend time getting the "feel" of the period before buying. **Books** (see p.62), **museums, specialist retail outlets** (see p.61), **collectors' clubs**, and **vetted fairs** (i.e. those where exhibitors have been professionally checked for their ability to date accurately and to spot authentic wares in good condition) will all help you to build up a picture of the overall field and prices, and perhaps help you decide on what you would like (and what you can afford) to collect. The choice is huge: you may want to collect wares by a particular designer or a specific factory, or designs in a particular form, such as cruet sets, sugar-shakers, or teapots. Another option is to collect on a specific theme – popular areas include nursery ware, chintzware, or novelties (anything from animal-shaped pots to tableware based on cinema stars). All of these categories offer an often bewildering range of prices, and for any budding collector a **reputable dealer** (a member of the **antiques associations** BADA – the British Antique Dealers' Association – or LAPADA – the Association of Art and Antique Dealers – or one who comes personally recommended) is probably your best investment. He or she should be able to answer your questions, provide you with a **written receipt**, and help you trade up as your tastes change, and may give advice on the tricky subject of **restoration**; however good, restoration will inevitably detract from the value.

Your very first piece makes you a collector. Once you have bought several pieces, you may need to make decisions about **display** and security. An Art Deco cabinet is ideal but often highly priced; open shelving, preferably mirror-backed to show off your collection to its full advantage, is a good alternative but will need dusting. Plates can be hung on the wall using plastic-coated plate hangers. Try to avoid direct sunlight falling onto hand-painted pieces, as this can cause fading. Avoid keeping fine china pieces anywhere that is likely to be subject to extremes of temperature, and any items that are not displayed should be packed in bubble-wrap and loosely taped, or wrapped in newspaper for protection.

**Security** is an ever-increasing risk, as prices for Art Deco pieces continue to rise. Separate **insurance** is advisable but can be costly. **Photographs** of your collection will help for insurance purposes as well as for selling or trading up, but make sure that you do not write your address on the back. Similarly, it is advisable to give your work address rather than your home address if you join a specialist collectors' club. Some collectors mark the base of their wares with their postal code using an invisible marker pen, although this can lead to confusion if a piece changes hands several times. Keep a **record of your collection** with details of the pieces, condition, where and when you bought each item, and the price you paid, both for your own information and to make sure that your insurance is adequate.

**Fakes** are also on the increase, as prices for Art Deco ceramics soar. Common sense, experience, and buying from a reputable dealer are the best protection. Never buy a piece if the circumstances seem remotely suspicious; **experience of handling** will help develop an almost instinctive appreciation of the subtle variations in colour, texture, and form that are the tell-tale marks of sophisticated fakes. Best of all, buy from a reputable dealer or from an auction house, so that you are assured of a written receipt that can be referred to should problems arise.

Above all, **enjoy your collection and collecting**. Do not be disheartened by high prices or the scarcity of good pieces, and be persistent in your search for that elusive treasure, as much of the enjoyment lies in the hunt. Buy the very best pieces you can afford, but buy what you like for a guaranteed long-term investment in pleasure if not money.

---

**Prices and dimensions**

Prices for antiques vary, depending on the condition of the item, geographical location, and market trends, so the price ranges given throughout this book should be seen as guides to value only.

Abbreviations used for dimensions are as follows: **ht** height; **l.** length; **w.** width; **diam.** diameter. Dimensions are given in both centimetres and inches.

# Clarice Cliff

Clarice Cliff (1899–1972) is probably the best-known English designer of Art Deco ceramics. After leaving school at 13 and working for several Staffordshire pottery firms, she joined A.J. Wilkinson Ltd (est. 1896) in 1916. In 1920 the company acquired the nearby Newport Pottery, and Cliff was given a free hand with its stock of old-fashioned white ware. She designed brightly coloured, geometric patterns, which transformed Newport's standard white wares into the "Bizarre" range, with its distinctive "honey" glaze. Originally launched in 1928 as cheerful, inexpensive domestic pottery, "Bizarre" was a huge success and paved the way for the vast array of shapes and patterns Cliff went on to produce.

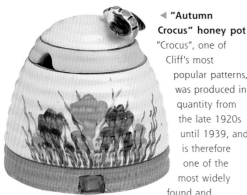

◀ **"Autumn Crocus" honey pot**
"Crocus", one of Cliff's most popular patterns, was produced in quantity from the late 1920s until 1939, and is therefore one of the most widely found and affordable patterns today. By 1934 it was available in different colour schemes – "Spring" (with pastel pink, blue, and green flowers), "Autumn" (shown here), "Sungleam" (with orange and yellow flowers, see right), and the more rare "Blue" (with blue flowers) and "Purple" (with purple flowers). This honey pot – part of the "Bizarre" range – was produced in two sizes, always with a bee on the lid.

"Autumn Crocus" honey pot, c.1933, ht 9.5cm/3¾in, **£295–355**

▼ **"Sungleam Crocus" sabot**
This sabot (or clog) – an unusual addition to the "Bizarre" range – is decorated with the "Crocus" pattern in the "Sungleam" colour scheme (orange and yellow). These sabots, which were inspired by Dutch clogs, were made in three sizes and designed to hold cacti. The shape is not readily found, and sabots are therefore rare and correspondingly highly priced.

"Sungleam Crocus" sabot, c.1935, l. 11cm/4¼in, **£240–295**

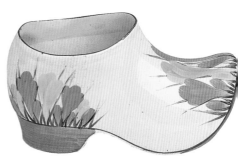

"Canterbury Bells" cruet set, c.1934, ht of salt pot 7cm/2¾in, £350–400

▶ **"Canterbury Bells" cruet set**
Cruet sets were produced in a wide range of patterns and shapes and are now highly collectable. Although technically a cruet set consists of a salt pot, a pepper pot, and a lidded mustard pot, salt and pepper pots are often collected as pairs on their own. The set shown above right is in the "Canterbury Bells" pattern, which was produced in two freehand-painted colour schemes (the alternative version featured blue, yellow, and purple flowers), both with a stippled ground. Avoid pieces in this pattern with a solid ground, as this probably indicates inappropriate restoration.

**MARKS**
Most wares are marked. Watch out for marks on a crackled glaze, as this may indicate a fake.

NASTURTIUM
HAND PAINTED
Bizarre
by
Clarice Cliff
NEWPORT POTTERY
ENGLAND

◀ **"Nasturtium" vase**
Vases by Cliff are found in a myriad of shapes, sizes, and patterns, and are perennially popular with collectors. This example from the "Bizarre" range was produced in two sizes and is a particularly unusual and desirable shape. The all-over painted decoration combines both the floral "Nasturtium" pattern (found in this colour scheme only) and a stippled ground, but still allows areas of Cliff's characteristic "honey" glaze to be seen. With this shape the "turrets" are vulnerable; they should be checked for damage or repair, which should always be reflected in the price.

• Cliff designed over 500 shapes and 2,000 patterns; shape, pattern, and condition determine collectability.
• Particularly sought-after shapes include the "Conical" range with cone-shaped bowls, vases, and teaware with triangular handles or feet, as well as the "Bonjour" and "Stamford" ranges.
• Rare, desirable patterns include "May Avenue", "Appliqué", "Inspiration", "Sunray", "Mountain", and "Solitude".
• Novelties such as Cliff's sought-after "Age of Jazz" figures and her face masks are very desirable.

"Nasturtium" vase, c.1935, ht 20cm/8in, £495–575

### ▼ "Broth" plate

The most sought-after plates by Cliff are those that feature a complete pattern rather than part of a pattern – new collectors should check details in one of the many reference books on Cliff. Value is determined to a large degree by the quality of the painting, and the most desirable pieces are thickly painted with visible brushstrokes in deep luminous colours, as seen on this plate from the "Fantasque" range. "Broth" – named after the rounded shapes in the pattern that resemble blobs of fat on the surface of soup – was an early pattern; it was produced from the early to the mid-1930s in three colour schemes: as shown; red, black, and green; and green, blue, and mauve.

### ▼ "Coral Firs" jam pot

Cliff's early landscape designs always included a house or a roof, unlike her later designs such as the "Coral Firs" pattern shown here. Along with the rare "Blue Firs" (blue trees on a blue ground) and even rarer "Green Firs" (green and yellow trees on a yellow ground), this is one of Cliff's best landscape designs. With lidded shapes, check that the colours on the base and lid match; also check lids for damage, as they are vulnerable. Although it may be tempting to buy a pot without a lid in the hope of finding one later, resist the temptation, as finding a good match is usually impossible.

### ▼ "Flora" face mask

Ceramic wall decorations were all the rage in the Art Deco period, and one new form – probably inspired by the wooden African masks so fashionable at the time – was the ceramic face mask (see pp.54–5). All of Cliff's face masks are highly sought after, with the rare "Chahar" commanding a premium. Examples were made with hollow backs, in both matt and high-gloss glazes, and in a variety of colours and sizes. Damage to the back of the mask will not greatly affect the value, but avoid pieces with any flaws or restoration to the face itself.

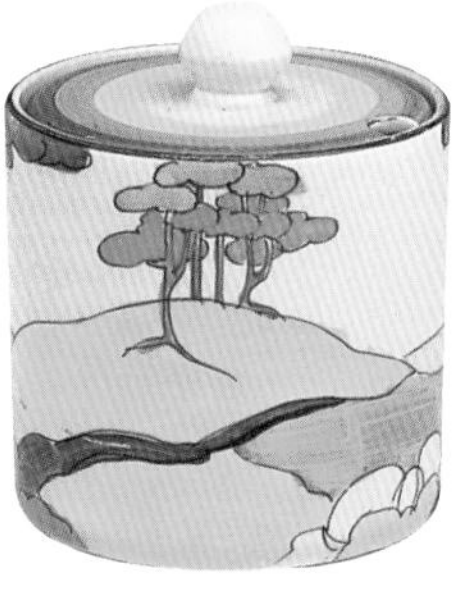

"Coral Firs" jam pot,
early 1930s,
ht 9.5cm/3¾in,
**£445–560**

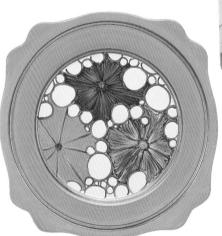

"Broth" plate, early 1930s, diam. 25cm/9¾in, **£525–650**

"Flora" face mask, 1932,
l. 15cm/6in, **£395–500**

"Circle Tree" tea-cup and saucer, early 1930s, ht of tea-cup 6.5cm/2½in, £450–500

• Look out for collectable pieces with deep, luminous colours and obvious brushstrokes.
• Check condition by looking and feeling for chips on delicate areas (rims, handles, spouts).
• Fakes are common. Tell-tale signs include washed-out colours, an uneven, slightly murky "honey" glaze, and a deliberately "aged" crackled glaze around the mark on the base.

## ▲ "Circle Tree" tea-cup and saucer

The tea-cup and saucer shown above are now highly collectable, as they were produced only for a short period due to problems with the conical shape. The earthenware body held the heat of the tea better than porcelain, but it was heavy and difficult to lift with the solid handle. The design was modified after c.1933, when the handle was given a small indentation to make lifting easier. Nevertheless, conical cups and saucers remain extremely popular with collectors, for whom the typical Art Deco shape, combined in this example with the equally typical Deco colours of orange, yellow, and black, far outweighs practical considerations. Cups and saucers must be in excellent condition for maximum value, although very minor damage such as a small chip will not detract too greatly from the value.

"Gardenia" vase, early 1930s, ht 20cm/8in, £1,100–1,300

## ▲ "Gardenia" vase

The innovative shape of this vase from the "Fantasque" range combined with the rare "Gardenia" pattern (also found in red and green) make this a very desirable piece. The top half of the vase was hand-painted; the bottom half would have been painted on a wheel, which would have created bands of colour – solid colour would suggest restoration. This design was also made as a jug in a larger size with a handle.

## ▼ "Secrets" sugar-shaker

Conical pieces are among the most desirable of all Cliff's shapes, and an added attraction with this example is the all-over pattern. However, the conical shape is fragile and should be checked for damage to the tip and to the holes, which may have been restored.

"Secrets" sugar-shaker, early 1930s, ht 13cm/5in, £650–750

# Susie Cooper

After training at Birmingham Art School, in 1922 Susie Cooper (1902–95) joined the Staffordshire firm of Gray's (*see* pp.28–9), where she designed geometric and floral patterns in enamel colours and lustre for hand-painted tableware. In 1929 she set up her own hand-painting business, and by 1932 she was also designing shapes; these were made in earthenware by Wood & Sons in Burslem, where Cooper had a production unit known as "Crown Works". Although she created an early range of abstract, geometric patterns in bright colours, the appeal of Cooper's work lies largely in her attractive yet functional range of shapes and in the understated charm of her floral patterns with their attention to detail and muted colours.

▼ **"Cubist" coffee-can and saucer**
This hand-painted coffee-can and saucer, originally part of a coffee-set that was also available in yellow, black, grey, and green, is a good example of one of Cooper's early geometric designs in a typical Art Deco style. Excellent condition is essential for cups and saucers, although crazing, to which pottery is particularly susceptible, is acceptable and will not detract from the value.

"Cubist" coffee-can and saucer, 1928–9, ht of can 5cm/2in, £85–150

▶ **"Cubist" chamber stick**
The unusual shape and vibrant all-over abstract pattern combine to make this chamber stick a highly collectable piece. However, the shape is fragile and should be checked for damage, which should be reflected in the price. Any signs of repainting would include subtle differences in colour and possibly a slightly rough texture where paint has been applied over the glaze. As the paint is lead based, any professional restoration should also use a lead-based paint.

"Cubist" chamber stick, 1928–9, diam. 13cm/5in, £185–250

• Pieces with underglaze transfer-printed patterns should never be restored with overglaze hand-painting as this will drastically reduce the value. Scratches or rubbed patches will also reduce the value.
• Complete tableware sets are rare. Individual pieces are much more affordable and can be added to over time.

"Homestead" sandwich tray, 1929, l. 31cm/12in, **£165–200**

"Kestrel" coffee-pot, 1930s, ht 23cm/9in, **£150–300** (complete set **£500–600**)

## ▲ "Homestead" sandwich tray

The success of the bright, colourful designs of Clarice Cliff (see pp.8–11) may have inspired the rare hand-painted landscape pattern shown on this sandwich tray – a typical Art Deco form. The set of square plates that would have accompanied such a tray is very rare, but the tray is still very collectable on its own. Many collectors hang trays on the wall so that the patterns can be seen to their full advantage.

## ▲ "Kestrel" coffee-pot

Cooper's designs were functional as well as attractive, as shown by this piece – originally part of a set, but very desirable on its own. The "Patricia Rose" pattern shown came in four colour schemes and is the most popular of Cooper's patterns applied by transfer – a technique she perfected, with the result that transfer-printed pieces are now as collectable as hand-painted ones.

## ▼ "Kestrel" trio

The pieces below were as practical as the coffee-pot shown left. The cup held the heat well and the handle was easy to hold. The pattern is "Dresden Spray", which was one of Cooper's many popular transfer-printed floral designs. It was made in various colour schemes – pink (most popular), green, yellow, and blue – and with bands of colour on the plate and cup rather than the shading shown in this example.

"Kestrel" trio, 1934, ht of cup 7cm/2¾in, diam. of saucer 15cm/6in, **£45–65**

MARKS

Most designs feature Cooper's signature, although exact marks vary. Wares made for Gray's may feature both the firm's galleon mark and Cooper's name.

HAND
GRAY'S POTTERY
HANLEY · ENGLAND
DESIGNED BY
SUSIE COOPER

# Keith Murray

Although New Zealand-born Keith Murray (1892–1981) trained as an architect, he is now equally well known as a designer of glass, silver, and, most notably, ceramics, which clearly show the influence of his architectural background. From 1933 he worked as a freelance designer for the Staffordshire firm of Wedgwood (est. 1759), where he produced designs that emphasized form rather than decoration for a range of predominately handmade wares. His designs include commemorative ware, tableware, and such small domestic items as ashtrays, beakers, cigarette boxes, and inkstands. However, most Murray devotees focus more on the designer's highly sought-after bowls and vases in distinctive modernist shapes, which are enhanced only by monochrome glazes (matt, semi-matt, or celadon) and engine-turned decoration.

▼ **Coffee-can and saucer**

Cups and saucers are a good starting-point for collectors, as they are reasonably priced and more readily available than bowls or vases. The moulded coffee-can shown here has all the hallmarks of Murray's style – a geometric shape decorated only with ribbing, a monochrome glaze, and no extraneous decoration other than the mercury silver handle (rarer and more collectable than a plain handle).

Coffee-can and saucer, 1933, ht of can 5cm/2in, £35–65

▶ **Celadon vase**

The high-gloss glaze used on this early earthenware vase is not usually associated with Murray, although the clean lines and incised decoration are typical of his work. This shape, which nearly always carries the full Murray signature, is also found in brown and white and in a larger size (ht 25.5cm/10in). Although clearly influenced by the Modernist architecture of the 1930s, the minimalist design is timeless, and its appeal is not limited purely to collectors of Art Deco wares.

Celadon vase, 1938, ht 18cm/7in, £140–200

Conical bowl, 1937, ht 10cm/4in,
**£135–200**

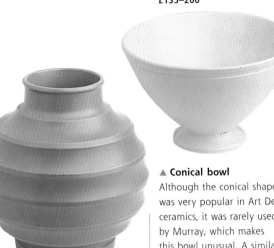

Engine-turned vase, 1935,
ht 28cm/10¾in, **£395–500**

## ▲ Engine-turned vase
Produced over a period of
about 12 years, vases in this
shape are among the most
collectable of Murray's designs.
Little of his work was suitable
for mass-production, and
typically this piece was hand-
thrown and then decorated on
an engine-turned lathe to give
the distinctive ridges, which
on early pieces often have a
white tinge. This design was
made in four sizes and various
colours – "straw", white,
"Moonstone" (greyish white),
green, and, rare and collectable,
blue and grey. As on all of
Murray's designs, any damage
is clearly visible and will affect
value, as restoration is difficult
and often all too evident.

## ▲ Conical bowl
Although the conical shape
was very popular in Art Deco
ceramics, it was rarely used
by Murray, which makes
this bowl unusual. A similar
version was produced without
a pedestal foot but with the
more characteristic ribbed
decoration. Other colours
included "straw", green, and,
most collectable, blue and
grey. The example featured
above comes complete with
original documents proving
that it was bought from
Wedgwood as a wedding
present for one of the firm's
employees. Such written
evidence, known as "proof of
provenance", not only acts as
authentication but also adds
to the interest of a piece;
collectors are therefore
advised to keep any original
packaging and invoices.

**FACT FILE**

• Bowls and vases are
most desirable, with
black and bronze
(basalt) vases being very
rare; tableware and
commemorative wares
are also high quality but
more reasonably priced.
• Good condition is
essential with such
pared-down shapes and
monochrome glazes.
• Damage beneath the
foot is acceptable, as
are minute chips, but
restoration is not. Poor
restoration can give
a slightly abrasive
"sandpapery" feel to the
glaze, so check by feeling
as well as looking.
• Check the interiors
of wide-necked vases or
bowls, where the colour
may have faded; any
discoloration must be
reflected in the price.
• Although fakes are
virtually unknown, some
SylvaC shapes (*see* pp.40–
41) are similar; however,
all SylvaC ware is marked
with the company name.

**MARKS**

Most wares are marked
either with Murray's
full signature and the
Wedgwood mark in
black or blue, or rubber-
stamped with "KM".

# Other famous designers

Many leading factories commissioned designs from fine-art painters in the 1920s and 1930s, and talented pottery dynasties also played an important role in ceramic design. Clarice Cliff (*see* pp.8–11) commissioned designs from the artist Dame Laura Knight for the firm of A.J. Wilkinson Ltd, and Charlotte Rhead, daughter of Frederick Alfred Rhead and sister of Frederick Hurten Rhead, designed hand-painted wares for Burgess & Leigh and the Crown Ducal range of A.G. Richardson & Co. The celebrated potter William Moorcroft made richly decorated, hand-thrown pottery with his son Walter at their Staffordshire factory, while Wedgwood approached the artist and illustrator Eric Ravilious to design tableware and the modeller and sculptor John Skeaping to design animal figures.

▶ **"Circus" plates by Dame Laura Knight**

Knight's fascination with the circus is reflected in both her paintings and her ceramic designs. Commissioned by Cliff, Knight (1877–1970) produced patterns for the "Circus" range of tableware for Wilkinson, which included teapots, sugar-bowls, hot-water jugs, coffee-pots with acrobats as handles, and even lamp-bases. However, "Circus" pieces are extremely rare, and collectors are unlikely to find examples other than the plates shown here. Ranging from 15cm to 46cm (6–18in) in diameter, they feature transfer-printed and hand-painted decoration and a gold-leaf surround. The decoration in the centre of the plate reflects the variety of acts found in a traditional circus.

"Circus" plates, 1931, diam. 23cm/9in, from **£500–700** (each)

"Persian Rose" vase,
c.1930s, ht 14.5cm/5¾in,
£185–250

▲ **"Persian Rose" vase by Charlotte Rhead**

A highly talented designer, Rhead (1885–1947) produced a range of shapes and patterns for chargers, wall plaques, and vases. The Crown Ducal vase shown here is a good example of her hand-painted, typically brightly coloured designs that were sometimes worked on by as many as eight or nine people. All pieces are marked; this vase carries the "C. Rhead" signature in a faint, tube-lined mark, together with the transfer-printed factory mark.

"Byzantine" wall plaque,
c.1932, diam. 31cm/12in,
£230–260

▲ **"Byzantine" wall plaque by Charlotte Rhead**

"Byzantine" was a popular stylized floral pattern designed by Rhead for the Crown Ducal range and applied to various forms, including the wall plaque shown here. The Art Deco fashion for ceramic wall ornaments included the more traditional shapes such as plaques as well as the newer forms such as face masks (see pp.54–5). The flat, open surface displays the skill of the designer and hand-painters to best advantage, but flaws, damage, and poor restoration are easily visible, so good condition and top-quality restoration are essential.

**FACT FILE**

• Signed pieces by Cliff, Knight, Charlotte Rhead, the Moorcrofts, Ravilious, and Skeaping (*see* pp.18–19) are very sought after.

• Where decoration rather than form is the biggest attraction, wares must be in top condition with no scratching or rubbing.

• Designs by Knight are extremely rare. Charlotte Rhead and the Moorcrofts were more prolific as they were full-time ceramicists.

• Early examples by Charlotte Rhead have a tube-lined "C. Rhead" signature. Later wares have a transfer mark of her full signature.

• Dating pieces by Ravilious can be problematic. Although his designs were created in the 1930s, many were not put into full production until the 1950s.

**MARKS**

"Circus" tableware is marked with the names of Knight, Cliff, and Wilkinson along with the range and date of the first edition.

### "Anemone" pot by Walter Moorcroft

This wheel-thrown earthenware pot was designed by Walter Moorcroft (b.1917), who worked with his famous father William Moorcroft (1872–1945) at the family factory in Staffordshire. The rich, dark blue ground (a very popular colour with collectors) and hand-painted floral "Anemone" pattern are typical of the factory's Art Deco designs. This pot carries the impressed "Moorcroft Made in England" mark, together with the signature of Walter Moorcroft, whose work is generally more affordable than that of his father and is therefore a good starting-point for new collectors. The most valuable Moorcroft Art Deco designs include the "Hazeldene" landscape patterns in "Moonlit Blue" (deep blues and greens) and "Eventide" (autumnal colours).

### "Wisteria" vase by William Moorcroft

The "Wisteria" pattern shown on this two-handled vase is a typical Moorcroft design featuring fruit, flowers, and leaves. The vase is signed "William Moorcroft", and this celebrated and sought-after signature explains the vase's high value. In the early 1930s designs based on fish were widely used, and Moorcroft reverted to a more muted palette, using beiges and greys, often with a salt glaze. Restoration on Moorcroft pots is so common that it is now acceptable, provided that it is of high quality and reflected in the price.

### "Travel" plate by Eric Ravilious

This plate is one of several designs commissioned by the Staffordshire firm of Wedgwood (est. 1759) from Ravilious (1903–42) in the 1930s, although many were not put into full production until the 1950s, several years after the designer's death. Created c.1937, "Travel" featured trains, boats, planes, and balloons transfer-printed in black on a Queen's Ware body and hand-tinted with turquoise on-glaze enamel. Ravilious's delicate, linear designs have a particularly English charm and are now highly sought after, especially those on such traditional English themes as "Boat Race Day", "Afternoon Tea", "Garden Implements", and "Garden".

"Travel" plate, designed late 1930s, diam. 18cm/7in, £75–95

"Wisteria" vase, c.1925, ht 20cm/8in, £1,000–2,000

"Anemone" pot, c.1930, ht 10cm/4in, £180–200

## ▼ "Alphabet" plate by Eric Ravilious

The success of nursery-ware ranges by other major manufacturers (see pp.52–3) led Wedgwood to commission the "Alphabet" design from Ravilious. The range was originally derived from the highly popular "Alphabet" mug, on which intricate motifs were accompanied by their initial capital letters. The "Alphabet" plate shown below features the minute attention to detail that young children find so intriguing, which is also very typical of Ravilious.

## ▼ "Seals" by John Skeaping

Skeaping (1901–80) also worked for Wedgwood, designing a range of stylized animal figures in two sizes, including kangaroos (now very rare), monkeys, seals, lions, wildebeest, and polar bears. They were made in a range of bodies, including black basalt and Queen's Ware, and colours (notably cream, celadon, "Moonstone", tan, and white), and were designed both with and without wooden plinths. The early, most collectable versions were usually in a matt glaze and were impressed with the Wedgwood mark and Skeaping's name. Wedgwood reissued the range, and later versions can be identified by the exclusive use of a high-gloss glaze and by the stamped name of the company without the Skeaping signature.

- Most Moorcroft wares show some signs of restoration. However, if professionally carried out, restoration should not detract too greatly from the value.
- Moorcroft miniatures are extremely rare and sought after.
- Decoration rather than form is the major appeal of Ravilious's designs, and it must therefore be in perfect condition, with no scratching or rubbing.
- Full tableware services are rarely found, but many enthusiasts collect piece by piece in the hope of forming a full service over time.
- Some of Skeaping's animal designs have fitted wooden stands. If the fit is very tight, do not attempt to pull the stand off as this may crack the figure. A professional should be able to help.

"Alphabet" plate, 1937, diam. 20cm/8in, **£80–100**

Left to right: white seal, c.1930s, ht 23cm/9in, **£225–350**; black seal, c.1930s, ht 17.5cm/7in, **£400–600**

# Burleigh Ware

Burleigh Ware is the name given to pottery manufactured by the firm of Burgess & Leigh (est. 1851). From the late 1880s the company was based in Middleport, Staffordshire, where it produced a wide range of earthenware designs including cottage ware and novelties (*see* pp.56–9). Hand-painted jugs in quirky, original designs with handles in the form of animals were extremely popular when first launched in the 1930s and are still very sought after today. Rarer, and correspondingly more highly priced, are jugs from the "Sporting" range, which reflect the great passion in the 1920s and 1930s for outdoor activities.

▼ **Jug**
This moulded and hand-painted earthenware jug is one of Burleigh's more understated Art Deco designs, although the characteristic black dots around the rim are still a major feature. The yellow version shown here is more desirable than the blue and green-and-white versions of the same design, as yellow is a more typical Art Deco colour. Collectors should check carefully for damage to handles and spouts, which may have been restored. Black paint is particularly vulnerable to flaking and "blooming", so watch out for any areas that have been retouched with either paint or even a felt-tip pen.

▼ **"Parrot" jug**
The humorous design of "Parrot" jugs makes them a highly popular collecting niche. The hand-painted parrot-shaped handles and the body design vary in colour and detail from jug to jug, and many collectors concentrate on acquiring as many different versions as possible. The "parrots" are easily damaged, especially the heads and crests, and restoration, although acceptable, will lead to a reduction in price.

"Parrot" jug, c.1930s, ht 23cm/9in, **£75–120**

Jug, c.1930s, ht 20cm/8in, **£95–130**

• As all jugs were hand-painted, the quality of decoration and originality of design will determine appeal and value.
• Rarity is not the prime consideration with animal jugs. Certain animals – rabbits, squirrels, parrots, and kingfishers, for example – although not necessarily rare, are very popular with collectors, many of whom concentrate on collecting different versions of one animal.

"Golf" jug, c.1930s, ht 23cm/9in, £650–800

"Sloth" jug, 1930s, ht 8cm/3in, £85–120

▲ **"Sloth" jug**

Many different animals appeared on Burleigh jugs, including flamingos, kingfishers, squirrels, monkeys, and dragons as well as the unusual sloth shown here. This, the smaller of two versions, may have been part of a tea-set, which also comprised a sugar-basin and a teapot – all of which are sought after and very rare. A taller version of the jug (23cm/9in) was also produced. Sometimes the animal formed part of the body of the jug as well as the handle; on the popular "Kingfisher" jug, for example, the bird swoops down onto the body of the jug to catch a fish, and on the "Kangaroo" jug the animals hop around the base.

▲ **"Golf" jug**

The "Sporting" series of jugs, which includes golfers, cricketers, and tennis players, appeals to both collectors of jugs and fans of sporting memorabilia. Burleigh jugs were all hand-painted by individual decorators, which guarantees a wide variety of details and facial expressions. The golfer in checked trousers above is more desirable than the one with plain trousers.

**MARKS**

All jugs are marked on the base. The early backstamp, used until c.1935–6, is as shown, often also with an artist/designer's mark.

"Harvest" jug, c.1930s, ht 13cm/5in, £65–95

▲ **"Harvest" jug**

"Harvest" jugs are among the most affordable animal jugs. The example shown above features a rabbit in a cornfield with stylized blue cornflowers; this design was also produced with red poppies. The jug came in two sizes: the smaller size shown here and a 17.5cm (7in) version.

21

# Carlton Ware

Carlton Ware was manufactured by the Staffordshire-based firm of Wiltshaw & Robinson (1890–1989). Production ranged from moulded earthenware teaware and salad ware decorated with fruit and flowers to high-quality gilded designs and lustre ware, advertising novelties, jewellery and cigarette boxes, napkin holders, and lamp-bases. With such a prolific and varied range, there is usually both a style and a price to suit most collectors. Large enamelled and gilded vases are very sought after by Carlton Ware enthusiasts and correspondingly highly priced; novice collectors may choose to begin with smaller items of tableware that can be added to over time.

◀ "Chinoiserie" vase

This vase is a good example of the highly collectable enamel-and-lustre range of vases produced by Carlton in the 1920s. The dark blue, high-glaze ground is decorated with hand-painted, heavily enamelled motifs and gilding to create a typical pseudo-Chinese effect known as "chinoiserie". Note that the inclusion of the barge in the pattern is unusual. Wear to the gilding on such areas as the rim, base, and handle should be reflected in the price, as re-gilding is expensive; however, it is worth the expense with such highly sought-after pieces.

▼ "Rouge Royale" jug

The "Royale" range included vases, dishes, trays, plates, and ginger jars, and came in a variety of colours, of which *rouge* ("red") is the most popular with collectors. The eye-catching shape, practical handle, good condition, and, above all, high-quality hand-enamelled and hand-gilded decoration of the popular "Humming Bird" pattern (also known as "Bird in Flight") all contribute to the collectability of this piece.

"Chinoiserie" vase, c.1920s, ht 31cm/ 12in, £395–500

"Rouge Royale" jug, 1925, ht 19cm/7in, £395–450

### ▼ "Sunflower" vase

The hand-painted "Sunflower" pattern with an unusual painted ground was designed both with (most collectable) and without a butterfly. "Sunflower" was used on a variety of shapes, including jugs and dishes, all of which are sought after by collectors. Such large pieces as this vase with a gilded rim are extremely collectable, but they are rare and correspondingly highly priced.

"Sunflower" vase, 1925, ht 25.5cm/10in, **£500–850**

"Handcraft" vase, 1925, ht 10.5cm/4in, **£295–400**

### ▲ "Handcraft" vase

Certain ranges such as "Handcraft" were only made for a limited period of time and are therefore rare and sought after. This example with a matt turquoise glaze came in four sizes, all decorated with enamels and gilding; other versions were produced with different ground colours and a high glaze. The range carries the written mark "Handcraft" in blue, together with an impressed shape number, a painted pattern number, and, in some cases, a gilder's mark.

**MARKS**

The mark shown below, which is found on the "Chinoiserie" vase, was replaced from *c*.1925 by a script signature (*see* pp.24–5).

(*see* pp.24–5).

"Handcraft" vase, 1925, ht 15cm/6in, **£350–450**

- Pieces such as vases and ginger jars with a large surface for decoration are very popular with collectors.
- Professional re-gilding is costly but usually worthwhile on such valuable pieces. However, avoid poorly restored examples where the new "gilding" (often gold paint and glaze) does not match the original.
- A worn or cracked glaze, worn ground colour, and any damage to the on-glaze, hand-enamelled decoration will reduce the value.
- Fakes are known, but the differences in colour and decorative detail are difficult to spot. The best protection is to buy from a reputable source.

### ▼ "Handcraft" vase

Although Carlton produced a range of wares decorated with geometric patterns in the 1920s and 1930s, for example the vase shown left, such wares are now rare and very collectable. This hand-painted example has a satin glaze and was made in three sizes, of which this is the smallest; the two larger sizes are sometimes found with handles.

"Fruit Basket" sugar-shaker, c.1930s, ht 13cm/5in, **£65–95**

"Foxglove" beaker, 1930s, ht 10.5cm/4in, **£75–85** (with lid **£100–115**)

Below: "Apple Blossom" cheese dish, 1930s, ht 10cm/4in, **£145–165**; "Apple Blossom" vase, 1930s, ht 13cm/5in, **£95–120**

### ▲ "Fruit Basket" sugar-shaker

In the 1930s Carlton produced "Fruit Basket" as a range of inexpensive, brightly coloured tableware for everyday use. The base colours were a strong green and a chrome yellow that contrasted with the bright colours used on the moulded decoration. The novel design and bright colours that were so popular in the 1930s make "Fruit Basket" equally sought after by today's collectors. Although the original modest prices no longer apply, the firm's tableware is much less highly priced than its lustre or geometric vases, and can be an attractive self-contained area for collectors with a limited budget.

### ▲ "Foxglove" beaker

This "Foxglove" beaker would originally have had a lid, incorporating three raised bumps in the pattern. When removed, the lid could be turned upside down and used as a saucer. Although ingeniously designed, these lids were highly vulnerable and are now rarely found, so beakers complete with lids are highly sought after. The pale green example seen above was also produced in a pale yellow – a marked contrast to the strong green and yellow used in "Fruit Basket" shown above left. Alternative colours were used only on export pieces and are very rare.

### ▲ "Apple Blossom" cheese dish and vase

Tableware featuring the "Apple Blossom" pattern is among the most popular Carlton Ware. The pattern was produced in quantity (from c.1936 to 1940) and in the two colour schemes shown here, which means that it is relatively easily found and collectors can gradually build up complete table settings. The depth of the relief leaf moulding varies, but designs with shallow-relief moulding will not necessarily be lower in value than designs with moulding in high relief. The value is only greatly affected if the moulding is damaged or absent.

"Redcurrant" jam pot,
1930s, ht 5cm/2in,
**£75–95**

## ▲ "Redcurrant" jam pot

The most sought-after Carlton jam pots are those complete with their original matching ceramic spoons and still in their original boxes. The base of the box was always marked with details of the contents, including the shape and pattern, so it is easy to check whether the box is authentic. Although the jam pot shown here does not have a spoon, it does have a lid (essential to value), and the lid knob is undamaged. This pot was produced in many different shapes and colours; examples with yellow bases were known as "Redcurrant", those with green bases as "Blackcurrant".

## ▼ "Cherries" jug

Unlike "Apple Blossom", the "Cherries" pattern is rare, so any piece featuring it is unusual and highly collectable. The jug shown below came in three sizes and was also produced with a yellow ground. All Carlton moulded tableware was designed for everyday use, and any pieces that have survived constant handling will need to be carefully checked for damage. A minor chip, particularly one that is not immediately visible, is acceptable, but hairline cracks are not and should be reflected by a reduction in the price.

"Cherries" jug, 1930s,
ht 10cm/4in, **£95–120**

• Carlton moulded earthenware tableware was produced in quantity for everyday use. It is therefore readily available, and collectors should be able to build up complete sets.

• Patterns that were popular when first brought out, such as "Apple Blossom", were produced for longer periods than less popular ones and are therefore more readily found and easier to collect. Rare patterns such as "Cherries" are highly sought after but difficult to find.

• With any pieces that were produced in quantity, good condition is crucial. Check carefully for restoration to areas such as handles, lid knobs, teapot spouts, jug lips, and any decorated areas in high relief.

• Boxed sets are very sought after. Empty boxes, which collectors can find and fill, are clearly marked on the underneath with details of the original contents.

From c.1930 much of Carlton's embossed tableware was marked as shown; some pieces also feature an impressed pattern number.

# Crown Devon

Crown Devon was the trade name used by the family firm of S. Fielding & Co., founded in Stoke-on-Trent in 1873 by Simon Fielding and rescued from bankruptcy five years later by Fielding's son Abraham. Under the directorship of the latter the company prospered and expanded, developing a prolific, highly collectable range of moulded earthenware tableware, salad ware, novelties, and figures. Abraham's son Ross took over the business in 1932, and production continued until the factory closed in 1982. Vases, dishes, and wall plaques in innovative shapes with hand-painted decoration ranging from florals to fantasy landscapes are all highly sought after by collectors.

"Orient" vase, late 1920s, ht 23cm/9in, £750–1,000

◀ **"Orient" vase**

Introduced in the mid-1920s, "Orient" is one of Crown Devon's finest patterns. With geometric motifs in brilliant, contrasting, hand-painted colours (red, black, and white is the other colour scheme), which are set off by gilding, it exemplifies the exotic face of Art Deco, and was used on a range of pieces including coffee-sets, lamp-bases, ginger jars, vases, and pen holders, all of which are stunning. This vase came in four sizes. Check the interiors of shaped pieces for discoloration as well as the condition of the gilding.

▼ **Pot-pourri holder**

The holder shown below, which combines an exotic oriental form with hand-enamelled decoration, is an unusual piece for Crown Devon in both shape and function. Such an ornamental piece is particularly prone to damage. The three gilded feet and the lid, with its pointed knob and gilding, are important areas to check, as is the enamelled decoration applied onto the matt-glazed, black ground. The piece is marked underneath in gilt with the Crown Devon mark as described opposite.

Pot-pourri holder, 1920s, ht 15cm/6in, £295–400

Tube-lined vase, 1930s,
ht 10.5cm/4in, **£165–200**

Floral jug, 1930s, ht 17.5cm/7in,
**£75–95**

FACT FILE

• Wares in innovative
Art Deco shapes and
vibrant colour schemes
attract the most interest.
• Items combining a
matt glaze and on-glaze,
hand-painted decoration
are very sought after.
• Collectors with a
limited budget can find
pieces from the more
affordable tableware
ranges in moulded
earthenware, although
the top condition
essential for everyday
wares is rare.
• Vases often resemble
costlier Wilton or
Carlton Ware designs.

## ▲ Tube-lined vase

The shape of this tube-lined
vase was popular in the
1930s, and several leading
factories including Carlton
produced similar versions.
Crown Devon's vase was
produced in four sizes, all
with a matt ground and
hand-painted decoration.
Tube-lining was so rarely used
on Crown Devon wares that it
is possible that this vase was
a sample. The tube-lining
has been used to create the
spider's-web pattern and part
of the floral decoration – an
unusual combination of motifs,
although pieces with spider's-
web patterns are sought after.

## ▲ Floral jug

This typically shaped Crown
Devon jug was made with
a huge variety of floral and
geometric hand-painted
designs in both primary and
pastel colours. Some examples
were decorated on the front
only, others on both sides.
This jug was one of Crown
Devon's more utilitarian
everyday tablewares, and with
such reasonably priced pieces
top condition is vital. However,
crazing on the high glaze
is acceptable, as is a small
chip to the underneath
of the base.

## ▼ Sweet dish

The pattern of a rural scene
used on this dish was featured
on many different forms,
including jam pots and mint
dishes. Here it has been given
a new dimension by the
ingenious use of the handle
as a bridge over a river. An
intact handle, as shown here,
is important for maximum
value but rarely found, as
these dishes were intended
for everyday use and the
handles were often damaged.

Sweet dish, 1930s,
w. 20cm/8in, **£70–90**

MARKS

Wares are marked
"Crown Devon" with an
elaborate crown. Some
designs also feature the
mark of the artist.

# Gray's

A.E. Gray Ltd (est. 1907; now part of Portmeirion Potteries) was founded in Stoke-on-Trent by Albert Edward Gray (1871–1959) as a wholesale ceramic decorating business. One of Gray's slogans was "Colour is courage", and he built up a team of talented and influential designers including Susie Cooper (*see* pp.12–13), and skilled painters that put his motto into practice. The company is renowned for its imaginative patterns and good-quality hand-painting on moulded earthenware; most sought after by collectors today are wares with bold, beautifully painted floral designs, lustred examples, or pieces signed by a well-known decorator.

**▲ Floral plate**

Floral plate, late 1920s, diam. 26cm/ 10¼in, £150–180

Floral patterns were extremely popular in the 1920s and 1930s, but this example is unusual in that the colours are predominantly pastel. The fine all-over decoration and gilt trim (a silver trim was also used) mark this plate as a piece from one of Gray's de-luxe ranges. If the trim is scratched or worn, the value will be considerably reduced. Decorative plates were one of Gray's strongest lines.

**▼ Globe jug**

This chunky floral piece is the largest of a range of jugs that were also made with narrower bodies. The strong sponged and hand-painted floral pattern shown here in autumnal hues came in a variety of other colour schemes, including blues, lilacs, and pinks, and greens and yellows. The gold trim (silver was also used) on the rim and handle are features of Gray's de-luxe ranges (see also the floral plate shown left) and must be unblemished for maximum value. A colour was sometimes used in conjunction with the metallic trim.

Globe jug, 1920s, ht 14.5cm/5¾in, £95–170

"Trellis" fruit-bowl, 1928, diam. 22.5cm/ 8¾in, £75–115

▲ **"Trellis" fruit-bowl**
Although Gray's patterns do not usually have names, "Trellis", shown here, is an exception. Designed by Cooper, whose name is sometimes incorporated in the mark, "Trellis" was painted freehand without outlines. The handles, which are unpainted, feature relief decoration, and the base has a stamped and hand-painted mark, together with a decorator's mark and pattern number. The bowl was made in several sizes, and smaller versions were often used as nut bowls.

Sugar-shaker, 1930s, ht 13cm/5in, £75–115

▲ **Sugar-shaker**
Sugar-shakers are a very popular collecting niche. This rare and desirable example, with attractive, all-over, hand-painted and sponged decoration in bright colours, is made entirely of earthenware; later examples tend to have metal tops, which were easier to clean. The holes seem disproportionately large today, but their substantial size was intended to help prevent clogging. Plastic replacement plugs for the base are acceptable, while damage or restoration to the pouring holes is not.

• Gray's is known for the quality of its hand-painting and its original patterns in bold colours.
• Large, fully painted pieces with a minimum of sponging are in general most sought after by collectors.
• Wares should be in good condition. Damage or wear to the painting or gilding should be reflected in the price.
• The mark of a well-known designer or decorator – usually in the form of a hand-painted signature – will add to the appeal.

**FACT FILE**

Biscuit box, 1920s, ht 9cm/3in, £130–170

▲ **Biscuit box**
Although the coloured trim on this hexagonal biscuit box identifies it as part of an everyday range, the shape is rare and collectable. However, such an angular design is prone to damage and should be checked at the corners, knob, and underside of the lid. Check also that the freehand pattern lines up on the lid and base.

**MARKS**

All Gray's pieces are marked; exact details vary, but most are brightly coloured and include either a galleon, a liner, or a clipper.

HAND–PAINTED

GRAY'S POTTERY
HANLEY ENGLAND

# Myott

The Staffordshire factory from which Myott, Son & Co. developed was inherited by Ashley Myott in 1897. By the 1920s he and his brother had built up a thriving home and export market for moulded tableware. Alongside a traditional series of designs, Myott developed an Art Deco range of adventurous and original shapes, hand-painted in brilliant, contrasting colours, that has now become very collectable. Jugs, vases, and table centrepieces are the most popular wares, and the more inventive the shape – for example fan-shaped and pyramid-shaped vases – the more desirable the piece.

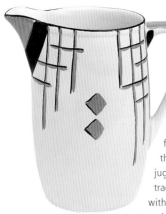

Geometric jug, 1930, ht 15cm/6in, £75–115

◀ **Geometric jug**
Designed for everyday use, this earthenware jug is in a shape traditionally associated with wash jug-and-basin sets and is one of the largest of a range of sizes. It is most notable for its geometric decoration, which although sparse is typical of the Art Deco period in design and colour. An alternative combination in green, blue, and black is equally desirable. Such a modest piece should be in tip-top condition, and collectors should check carefully around the spout, handle, and black rim.

▼ **Conical jug**
Far more typical of Myott jugs than the piece shown left is the conical earthenware jug with attractive, stylized geometric spout and handle shown below. The bright ground of orange, green, and yellow is particularly associated with the company, as is the sparsely scattered floral decoration. Although in general more densely painted patterns are most sought after, eye-catching shape, good condition and colour, and an affordable price make such a piece an excellent starting-point for a novice collector.

Conical jug, 1930s, ht 15cm/6in, £85–115

Long-necked jug, 1930s,
ht 20cm/8in, £85–115

Jug, from 1930s, ht 17cm/
6¾in, £85–120

FACT FILE

- Myott jugs and vases are a popular niche collecting area. The more original and inventive the shape, the more desirable the item.
- Good condition is crucial with hand-painted wares; restoration of any kind will detract from the value, although tiny chips on the base may be acceptable.
- Check rims by feeling as well as looking to detect rough areas that may indicate retouching.

## ▲ Long-necked jug

An all-over pattern and inventive shape identify this jug as a piece by Myott. The accentuated spout and handle are particularly distinctive, but they are vulnerable and must be checked for damage or restoration; tiny chips may be acceptable, especially if on the base, but repainting is not. The hand-painted pattern is in the earthy colours typical of Myott. This jug was made in two sizes, the one shown here and a taller, 25.5cm (10in) version.

## ▲ Jug

The inspiration for the deliberately crude shape of this unusual earthenware jug with its irregular wavy rim seems to be more medieval than Art Deco. The hand-painted pattern – probably inspired by the traditional harlequin or pierrot costume – was a favourite Art Deco motif, and here it has been applied in a deliberately crude style. The black base should be carefully checked for repainting, as should the rim and handle. Any scratches or wear to the hand-painting will detract from the value.

"Bowtie" vase, 1930s, ht 20cm/8in,
£135–165

## ▼ "Bowtie" vase

"Bowtie" vases – made only by Myott – are rare and desirable. They originally came with pierced, ceramic "frogs", which were fitted inside the vases to hold the flowers and sometimes numbered to identify the shapes. Designs with an all-over pattern (either floral or geometric) are most desirable. This shape was also produced with a handle, as a jug.

MARKS

Most Art Deco wares feature the mark with a crown, shown below. A painter's mark is sometimes also found.

# Poole Pottery

Poole Pottery was originally established in 1873 in Poole, Dorset, as Carter & Co. By 1921 the company was known as Carter, Stabler & Adams, and although early wares are now known as Poole Pottery, this did not become the official trading name until 1963. During the 1920s and 1930s the firm was particularly successful, producing a popular range of hand-thrown ornamental stoneware with floral and geometric patterns under a matt glaze and winning a prize at the Paris Exhibition of 1925. Many artists worked for Poole, most of whom marked their designs, and collectors should use a good reference book to identify the different marks used.

▼ **Coffee-pot with cup and saucer**
Although less densely patterned than many other wares of the 1920s, Poole's small coffee- and tea-sets – most of which were made for presentation purposes – are now rare and sought after. However, with time and patience a set can be built up.

▲ **"Leipzig girl" charger**
The stylized dancing nymph on this large charger was known as "Leipzig girl" and, like the pattern on the coffee-pot shown left, pre-dates the popular stylized floral designs by Truda Adams. Although slightly damaged on the rim, the size, unusual figurative pattern, and early production date make this rare piece highly collectable.

"Leipzig girl" charger, 1926–7, diam. 44.5cm/17in, **£800–900**

Left to right: cup and saucer, 1920s, ht of cup 8cm/3in, **£40–50**; coffee-pot, 1920s, ht 23cm/9in, **£65–75**

## ▼ Floral vase

While John Adams designed most of the Poole shapes of the 1920s, his wife Truda Adams (Truda Carter from 1931) created the patterns that were painted onto a matt-glaze ground. The vase shown below is an interesting example of a rare and early pattern incorporating the stylized flowers that were to become a hallmark of the company. Earthenware is easily chipped, and, although more robust than tableware, vases should be carefully checked for damage; any imperfections should always be reflected in the price.

Globe jug, 1930s,
ht 20cm/8in, £300–350

## ▲ Globe jug

The bulbous shape of this jug provides a large surface for the all-over pattern that is central to its appeal. Designed by Truda Carter and painted by Eileen Prangnell, one of Poole's highly skilled decorators, the pattern combines floral and geometric motifs. Vases such as this are particularly popular among collectors, so condition is important, especially as earthenware is difficult to restore. Pay particular attention to areas such as the handle, rim, and lip, which may be chipped or cracked.

**FACT FILE**

• Poole is a popular collecting niche, with its own collectors' club.
• Floral patterns in pastel colours on a matt ivory ground are among the most collectable pieces; plain wares are more modestly priced and are a good starting-point for new collectors.
• Look for pieces with hand-painted decoration with clean, crisp outlines and sharp definition.
• Condition is vital; restoration will reduce the value, as will visible damage. However, crazing is acceptable.

## ▼ "Bluebird" vase

Combining stylized floral and geometric motifs, and featuring the white base and lavender interior typical of Poole, "Bluebird" is one of the firm's most popular patterns. This vase shows the early version with the bird in flight; in later versions the bird sits on a twig.

"Bluebird" vase, 1930s,
ht 19cm/7½in, £125–160

Floral vase, c.1930,
ht 37cm/14in, £700–800

**MARKS**

Nearly all wares were marked on the base. Designs are marked "Carter, Stabler, Adams Ltd" or "Poole England".

# Royal Winton

Royal Winton – the trade name of Grimwades Ltd – was based at the Winton Pottery (est. 1885) in Stoke-on-Trent. The company manufactured a diverse range of tableware and decorative designs in moulded earthenware including lamp-bases, candlesticks, jug-and-basin sets, dressing-table sets, *jardinières* with stands, novelties, and cottage ware. In the 1930s Royal Winton became particularly renowned for its chintzware (*see* pp.48–9) – pretty, affordable tableware decorated with all-over floral patterns and produced in large quantities – which is becoming increasingly highly sought after worldwide. Royal Winton breakfast-sets and stacking tea-sets are also especially popular among collectors.

▼ **"Hazel" teapot**
Teapots are very popular with collectors, especially when combined with a top chintzware pattern, such as "Hazel" – seen here on a four-cup "Ajax" shape teapot (also made in two- and twelve-cup sizes). Restoration on chintzware is unacceptable except on the base, so all areas that are prone to damage, such as spouts, lids, knobs, and handles, must be checked carefully. The base of this teapot features an impressed mark for the shape, the company mark, and a transfer-printed mark of the pattern.

▼ **"Julia" butter-dish**
The lidded design from the "Ascot" range featured below would have been moulded, glazed, skilfully covered with the transfer-printed pattern – in this case, the highly sought-after "Julia" – and then reglazed. Although such "double glazing" is particularly susceptible to crazing, this will not detract from the value provided that, as in this case, the piece is otherwise in good condition, with no hairline cracks or hand-painted restoration.

"Hazel" teapot, 1934, ht 13cm/5in, £400–600

"Julia" butter-dish, late 1939, ht 12cm/4¾in, £295–400

"Richmond"
toast rack, 1938,
l. 18cm/7in, £225–260

## ▲ "Richmond" toast rack

Toast racks, which come in a variety of sizes and designs including three-bar and pierced styles, form a self-contained collecting niche as well as being highly sought after to make up breakfast-sets. Applying the transfer pattern to the irregular version shown above without leaving obvious joins would have demanded great skill – on later examples the bars are sometimes left plain. "Richmond" is not an especially rare pattern, but the combination of a gilt trim, a very desirable shape, and an all-over pattern makes this piece particularly collectable.

"Somerset" sweet dish, 1932,
ht 9cm/3in, £225–300

## ▲ "Somerset" sweet dish

The Royal Winton catalogue describes this shape as a "footed nut bowl", although it is generally known as a "sweet dish". The unusual shape (circular flatware was more common) and all-over "Somerset" pattern with a blue trim (some examples feature a gold trim) make it highly desirable. The join between the foot and the bowl should be checked for signs of restoration or cracks.

**FACT FILE**

- Rare shapes include teapots, hot-water jugs, lamp-bases, candlesticks, and biscuit barrels.
- Among the most sought-after patterns are "Evesham", "Hazel", "Julia", "Royalty", "Sweet Pea", and "Welbeck".
- Patterns must be crisp and clear for maximum value; check carefully for fading, scratching, or restoration with other patterns.
- If the pattern on an irregular shape has an obvious join, this will not detract from the collectability.

## ▼ "Sweet Pea" nut dish

Introduced in 1936, and designed with a pale yellow or chrome yellow ground with a gold or deep blue trim, "Sweet Pea" is highly sought after today. As with any chintzware pattern it should be checked for fading; the blue or pink areas are most likely to be affected and may fade to a greyish colour. This dish was manufactured both with (as shown) and without a divide down the centre.

"Sweet Pea" nut dish, 1936,
l. 25.5cm/10in, £135–200

**MARKS**

The circular mark shown below is found in blue, green, or black. On later pieces "Royal Winton" appears in script.

# Shelley

Shelley (1872–1966) was known in the 1920s and 1930s both for its high-quality tableware and for its go-ahead marketing strategies, including a national advertising campaign, the company's own magazine (the *Shelley Standard*), and the "Shelley Girl" – a fashionable young woman shown drinking from Shelley teaware. Production was prolific, consisting mainly of tableware with a high-quality translucent china body in distinctive shapes decorated with geometric designs, floral patterns, and landscapes. Most sought after by Art Deco collectors are the now rare and innovative "Vogue", "Mode", and "Queen Anne" ranges.

▼ **"Vogue" trio**

Although a superb shape, "Vogue" was produced only for a limited period (1930–33) because of its impractical design. The solid triangular handle was difficult to hold, and the wide rim meant that the tea cooled too quickly. However, to collectors "Vogue" is one of the most desirable Shelley shapes, and this slip-cast trio also has the added appeal of an unusual hand-painted pattern.

"Vogue" trio, 1930, ht of cup 5cm/2in, w. of plate 15cm/6in, **£250–300**

▼ **"Mode" trio**

With the "Mode" range, Shelley attempted to rectify some of the design faults of "Vogue". In order to retain the heat better, the china body was made thicker and the rim width was reduced. However, the handle was still solid and hard to hold, and this made "Mode" too impractical to justify a long production run – it was manufactured from 1930 until 1931. The rarity of this design makes it very desirable.

"Mode" trio, 1931, ht of cup 7.5cm/2¾in, w. of plate 15cm/6in, **£180–250**

## "Eve" trio

The "Eve" shape was produced over a much longer period (c.1932–8) than "Vogue" or "Mode", and is therefore more readily available to collectors. Although the handle of the tea-cup is still triangular, it is open and easy to hold. The characteristic fine china was decorated with a variety of patterns: floral and geometric designs, as well as variations on the transfer-printed and hand-painted country scene shown here.

## "Regent" trio

A further stage in the evolution of the Shelley tea-cup resulted in "Regent" – one of the firm's best-selling shapes, produced over a relatively long period (1932–9). Practicality triumphed over design as the cup in this range was given a round handle that is easy to hold. The yellow "Phlox" pattern shown here is one of hundreds of collectable hand-painted and transfer-printed patterns used on this shape. Square plates were produced in addition to the round plate shown below. The long period of production makes it possible to build up a complete set.

**FACT FILE**

• Certain patterns and colour schemes were made for export only; special order teaware may be found with interiors in a solid colour or gold.
• On more standard shapes, patterns in typical Art Deco colour combinations such as green, black, and silver or red, orange, and yellow (sometimes black) are very popular.

## "Queen Anne" trio

This shape has been popular ever since it was first registered in 1926. The panels on the cup are well suited to both the early hand-painted designs of flowers, gates, and garden scenes, and the hand-painted and transfer decoration, such as "Peaches and Grapes" shown here.

"Regent" trio, 1932, ht of cup 7.5cm/2¾in, diam. of plate 18cm/7in, **£75–95**

"Eve" trio, 1932, ht of cup 7.5cm/2¾in, w. of plate 15cm/6in, **£125–150**

"Queen Anne" trio, 1926, ht of cup 5cm/2in, w. of plate 15cm/6in, **£85–115**

### ▼ "Syringa" teapot

The teapot that accompanied the 21-piece tea-set in the "Regent" range was sold as an optional extra. This example in the unusual "Syringa" pattern was sold as part of a "tea-for-two" set, which also included a milk-jug, sugar-bowl, two cups and saucers, and a small plate for slices of lemon. The bases of "Regent" teapots nearly always have hairline cracks, but this should not deter collectors, especially those buying to complete sets for display rather than use. However, collectors should look out for damage to such vulnerable areas as spouts, handles, and lids.

### ▼ "Melody" vase

This vase is part of the Shelley chintzware range. The floral "Melody" transfer-printed pattern was produced with a hand-painted border in four different colours – pink, yellow, blue, and, most common, green. The vase was made in porcelain as well as in the earthenware shown here. All examples are rare and highly sought after to complement the factory's teaware. The backstamp carries the words "Shelley" in script inside a scalloped cartouche, together with a tiny sample of the pattern, the pattern name, and the decorator's mark.

### ▼ "Maytime" water-jug

"Maytime" is another of Shelley's popular transfer-printed floral patterns. An all-over design, it was combined with a hand-painted trim and was used on a wide range of shapes including china teaware, candlesticks, eggcups, hand-bells, and lamp-bases. As with the "Melody" vase shown below left, the pattern rather than the shape usually holds the greater attraction for collectors, so this piece with all-over decoration is very desirable. However, the pattern is easily damaged and should be checked for scratches, obvious joins, fading from exposure to direct sunlight, or wear from over-zealous washing.

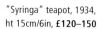

"Syringa" teapot, 1934, ht 15cm/6in, **£120–150**

"Melody" vase, 1930s, ht 18cm/7in, **£95–130**

"Maytime" water-jug, 1930s, ht 13cm/5in, **£95–115**

## ▼ "Harmony" ginger jar

The ginger jar was a very popular Art Deco shape, which lent itself to a variety of decorative treatments. This example, which came in several sizes, features the "Harmony" pattern, said to have begun life as a mistake by a painter but now a highly collectable design. The colours were poured or dripped onto the shape as it turned on the wheel, so creating the characteristic streaks. "Harmony" was produced in a variety of colour combinations, of which pink and grey are the rarest. The lid must be present and undamaged, so check carefully around the edge for cracks and chips as well as checking the rim of the jar itself.

## ▼ Napkin rings

Napkin rings were produced as singles or pairs, or in boxed sets of two, four, and six. Original boxed sets are rare and desirable, and collectors with limited budgets may prefer to collect singles in a variety of patterns. Condition must be tip-top, and moulded earthenware napkin rings with a foot, as shown here, should be checked carefully for damage. Napkin rings are not always marked, but if they are the mark is usually found on the inside.

Napkin rings, 1930s, diam. 7cm/ 2¾in, £70–80 for the pair (£40–50 each)

**FACT FILE**

• Shelley chintzware is rare and sought after by both Shelley fans and chintzware collectors.
• Pieces featuring delicate hand-painted patterns should be washed by hand.
• Hairline cracks are easily detected on fine, translucent china by holding the piece up to the light; restoration will show up as a grey area on the white body. Hairline cracks are sometimes "cleaned up" with bleach, so watch out for the characteristic smell. Although a hairline crack may be acceptable on pieces used for display only, a "sprung" crack (i.e. one into which a fingernail can be fitted) is never acceptable.
• Original packaging is a great bonus. Shelley boxes are usually plain and marked only with the company name.

**MARKS**

All authentic wares are marked, most commonly with the signature within a cartouche shown here. See also *The Shelley Guide* for information on marks.

"Harmony" ginger jar, 1930s, ht 25.5cm/10in, £185–250

# SylvaC

The firm founded in Stoke-on-Trent by William Shaw and William Copestake in 1894 first used the name SylvaC in the mid-1930s, by which time the company was producing tableware as well as the animal figures and ornaments for which it is best known today. SylvaC responded to the Art Deco demand for ornaments and wall decorations with a range of moulded and matt-glazed earthenware vases, posy holders, wall pockets, ashtrays, eggcups, and small animal figures in muted colours (including beige, blue, green, and brown). Although mass-produced and inexpensive in the 1930s, SylvaC pieces, especially the firm's animals, are rapidly increasing in value.

## ▼ Jug

Although produced in the 1930s, this jug has an almost Victorian feel to it and would have appealed greatly to contemporary buyers who had retained the traditional heavy furniture so popular in the mid to late 19thC. This piece was produced as an inexpensive jug in large quantities and in many different colours, including beige, grey, and blue. Such a modestly priced piece should be in top condition, as restoration might cost more than the jug itself; any damage should be reflected in the price.

Jug, c.1930s, ht 23cm/9in, **£35–50**

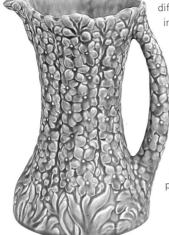

## ▼ Pixie wall pocket

Ceramic wall ornaments, ranging from face masks (see pp.54–5) to the wall pocket shown here, were all the rage in the 1930s. This example features winged pixies; rarer, and therefore more sought after, are SylvaC wall pockets decorated with fairies or elves (similar to pixies but without wings). Some examples feature squirrels or rabbits – the latter are probably most closely associated with this firm. Although the pockets are strongly modelled, the figures are fragile and should be carefully checked for damage or restoration.

Pixie wall pocket, 1930s, ht 15cm/6in, **£55–95**

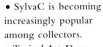

- SylvaC is becoming increasingly popular among collectors.
- Typical Art Deco shapes include posy holders, wall pockets, bookends, and matchstrikers.
- Early pieces with high-quality, detailed moulding are very desirable.
- Animals are keenly sought after, as are jugs with moulded handles in the shape of animals.
- Less elaborately moulded jugs are modestly priced and therefore a good starting-point for budding collectors.
- Most pieces are impressed on the base with the model number, the company name, and "England".

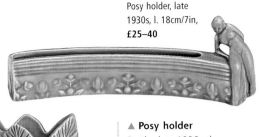

Posy holder, late 1930s, l. 18cm/7in, £25–40

## ▲ Posy holder

By the late 1930s the moulding and detail on SylvaC figures had become coarser, as seen on this posy holder – a popular Art Deco shape. Although the matt green of this example is highly characteristic of SylvaC production, the depiction of a naked woman is not – rabbits, squirrels, and pixies were far more typical – and this adds to the value of the piece. This posy holder was produced as one of a range and was also available in other colours; many enthusiasts will focus on building up a collection of as many different designs from the same range as possible.

Leaf vase, 1930s, ht 23cm/9in, £30–50

## ▲ Leaf vase

The irregular shape of the rim and the detailed moulding on the leaves are central to the appeal of this vase, which, like the green jug shown far left, would not have looked out of place in a Victorian parlour. This design was produced in a variety of colours, including beige, brown, and blue, all with a characteristic matt glaze. Such vases were mass-produced at modest prices and are still very affordable today, so collectors should avoid any examples with damaged or restored leaf tips.

## ▼ Scottie dog

SylvaC produced a large range of animals, which included many different breeds of dog in various colours. All of these dogs were well modelled, with close attention paid to such detail as hand-painted eyes and noses. Not only are they among the most popular of all SylvaC's ranges, they also appeal greatly to collectors of dog novelties. Other animals include rabbits, hump-backed cats, lambs, frogs, and hares.

Scottie dog, 1930s, ht 9cm/3in, £25–40

# Other major factories

Collectable utilitarian and decorative ranges were produced by a wide range of major factories in Britain and continental Europe in addition to those already discussed. Wares in unusual shapes, with eye-catching designs, are particularly sought after, as are pieces by well-known designers. Notable British factories include Maling and S. Hancock & Sons, both best known for their surface decoration. In continental Europe, factories such as Gouda in The Netherlands and Boch Frères in Belgium were generally more adventurous in exploring the Art Deco style, producing more strikingly innovative shapes and patterns than their British counterparts.

▼ **"Chinese Lanterns" wall plaque by Maling**
This decorative hand-painted and tube-lined earthenware wall plaque was made in four equally vivid ground colours, the most desirable of which is a mix of blue and pink. Tube-lining is susceptible to damage and needs careful examination. More modestly priced, but equally sought after, is the range of lustre ware by Maling (est. 1762).

"Chinese Lanterns" wall plaque, 1937, diam. 28.5cm/11in, £185–250

▶ **Double-handled vase by Gouda**
This double-handled, hand-painted earthenware vase is just one of many unusual shapes by Gouda (est. 1898), many of which were exported to Britain. Floral designs are typical. All pieces are clearly marked with hand-painted details of the pattern, plus the date and place of production. Although good condition is desirable, restoration is acceptable on Gouda pieces.

Double-handled vase, 1918, ht 22cm/8½in, £245–275

This is one of several marks used by Maling; most incorporate some variation on this fortress.

**MARKS**

## Geometric vase by Boch Frères

The firm of Boch Frères (est. 1767) manufactured some of the most important pieces of Belgian Art Deco ceramics. This striking, deeply moulded earthenware vase was designed by Charles Catteau (1880–1966), one of the company's leading designers, and bears his signature. It combines an innovative Art Deco shape with eye-catching decoration – a combination that has led the firm's work to achieve impressive prices at auction. Vases are very sought after, in particular early geometric patterns and shapes and pieces signed by designers.

## Vase by Hollinshead & Kirkham

Hollinshead & Kirkham (c.1870–1956), known as "H & K", produced a range of tableware, vases, plates, candlesticks, and boxes. Vases are most popular, especially the rare large examples. The vase below came in several sizes, and features H & K's typical high-gloss glaze and hand-painted fruit decoration on a beige-and-brown ground. Floral and geometric patterns were also used, as was a dark-blue-and-green ground. Condition should be very good, as the piece is modestly priced; however, crazing is acceptable.

FACT FILE

• The more modestly priced the piece, the more important the condition. Tableware must be in tip-top condition. However, on more exclusive pieces, such as those by Gouda, restoration is acceptable.

• Wares by British firms tend to be most sought after for good surface decoration.

• The adventurous shapes and patterns used on decorative wares by factories in continental Europe are often seen as more typically Art Deco and therefore most collectable.

## Toast rack by S. Hancock & Sons

The firm of Hancock (1857–1937) is noted for its hand-painted tableware, of which this earthenware toast rack from the "Ivory Ware" range is a good example. The shape, with two small dips for butter and jam, is typical of the 1930s, but the pierced rack is vulnerable and needs to be checked for restoration. Jam pots and "tea-for-two" sets are also popular but must be in good condition.

Geometric vase, 1930s, ht 36cm/14in, **£300–400**

Vase, c.1920s, ht 10cm/4in, **£35–45**

Toast rack, 1930s, l. 18cm/ 7in, **£55–75**

# Factories to watch

As the Art Deco collecting field has expanded, so the number of factories attracting interest from collectors has grown. Most British factories were based in Staffordshire, and increasingly popular moulded earthenware from this region includes the nursery designs of Wade, Heath & Co. Ltd decorated with characters from the animated films of Walt Disney (*see* pp.52–3), the ornaments, cottage ware, salad ware, and "Beatrix Potter" nursery ware of John Beswick Ltd, the ornamental garden designs of R.H. & S.L. Plant Ltd, and wares with floral decoration painted by the Radford Handcraft Pottery. The Longpark Pottery Co.'s Torquay ware (named after the firm's location on the South-west coast) is also growing in popularity.

▼ **Pinch jug by Longpark**
This jug is one of a range of Torquay wares made by, among others, Longpark (c.1903–57) that were originally designed as eye-catching yet inexpensive souvenirs but have recently become collectors' items. The range is also known as "motto" ware, as each piece features an incised motto in brown or green on the cream, green, or blue body. Chipping is not acceptable on mugs, jugs, and jam pots, but may be fine on unusual shapes such as loving-cups, biscuit barrels, and teapots. Pots in the darker clay used before the 1930s are most desirable.

Pinch jug, early 1920s, ht 9cm/3in, **£40–50**

▲ **"Sundial" butter-dish and teapot by Beswick**
Although better known for face masks (see pp.54–5) and novelties (see pp.56–9), Beswick (est. 1840) also produced tableware ranges. "Sundial", which came in this colour scheme only, was one of the firm's most popular patterns, but good condition is essential, as the sundial knobs are easily damaged. Matching teapot-stands were also made, and it is an added bonus if they are still present.

Above:
"Sundial" butter-dish, 1930s, ht 8cm/3in, **£65–85**;
"Sundial" teapot, 1930s, ht 15cm/6in, **£75–100**

*A stitch in time saves nine*

**MARKS**

"Sundial", one of Beswick's most innovative patterns, received the ultimate seal of approval from the royal household.

"SUNDIAL"
AS PURCHASED
BY
H.M. QUEEN MARY.

• This is a good starting-point for new collectors who can get the "feel" of the period without making costly mistakes.
• Most desirable are unusual pieces or those that typify the period by colour, shape, or theme.
• Check carefully for faded colours or damage to the glaze where pieces may have been washed with harsh detergents.

"Anemone" vase, late 1930s, ht 19.5cm/7¾in, £35–50

"Big Bad Wolf" jug, 1932, ht 27cm/10¾in, £750– 850 (musical version, from £750–950)

"Tuscan Garden", c.1930s, ht 13cm/5in, £95–115

▲ **"Anemone" vase by Radford**

Vases and posy bowls were produced in great quantity and variety by Radford (est. c.1933), and this example was made in several sizes and with different ground colours, including blue, green, fawn, and pink. The freehand decoration, which was painted under the matt glaze, is typical of Radford's production in the 1920s and 1930s; geometric patterns with gold or silver trims are more unusual, and consequently more highly priced. Unusual forms such as tall jugs and plaques also tend to be more valuable. Pieces are signed "Radford" or "E. Radford" and may also feature an artist's mark.

▲ **"Big Bad Wolf" jug by Wade**

This hand-painted jug is part of a highly popular range by Wade (est. 1810), which includes teaware, teapots, jugs, and sugar-bowls based on characters from Walt Disney films. Such designs appeal equally to collectors of Disney and of Art Deco. The jug shown above also came in a musical version with a wind-up musical movement in the base. When the key was wound and the jug lifted, the tune *Who's Afraid of the Big Bad Wolf?* would play. For maximum value the musical version must be in perfect working order.

▲ **"Tuscan Garden" by Plant**

The hand-painted "Garden" series by Plant (est. 1898) included bookends (collectable both in pairs and individually), sundials, and garden benches as well as at least 18 different garden designs. Although all of the gardens differ in style, each one features multi-coloured hollyhocks, a wall, and a hand-painted number referring to the individual garden design. Check carefully for damage to protruding areas.

# Figures

The ethereal Art Nouveau maiden of the late 19thC and early 20thC was transformed in the 1920s and 1930s into an independent young woman in fashionable clothes, often with bobbed hair, who made the most of the new freedom offered by the "Jazz" age. She was immortalized in a wide range of now highly collectable moulded and hand-painted porcelain figures. Manufacturers in continental Europe such as Katzhütte, Goebels, Rosenthal, Friedrich Goldscheider, and Lenci produced sinuous, elegant, stylized figures, which were generally better modelled and painted than those of their English counterparts (Crown Devon, Carlton, and Royal Doulton), whose figures are often in rather stilted poses.

▼ **Czech girl**

The delicate porcelain figure shown here was made as a blonde or brunette, with or without flowers in her hair, and in dresses of different colours and patterns. All versions were hand-painted, so features and facial expressions vary. Any prominent details should be checked for damage – heads and outstretched hands are particularly delicate, and hand-painted necklaces or bracelets (not usually found on this model) may conceal a join where heads or hands have been restored.

Czech girl, c.1930s, ht 25.5cm/10in, **£175–225**

▶ **Dancing girl by Katzhütte**

This German firm (est. 1762) is known for its production of figures with finely modelled and well-painted faces. This example came in various colours – green, blue, pink, yellow, and brown – and although in this case the girl is dancing, she also came in many different poses with a variety of accessories, and sometimes with a pet. This figure and the variation with a borzoi, both of which encapsulate the spirit of the "Jazz" age, are the most popular designs. Most were made with a white base; all feature the Katzhütte mark.

Dancing girl, c.1930s, ht 24.5cm/9in, **£395–495**

## ▼ Girl with a lyre by Goebels

Although better known for its novelty range, the firm of Goebels also produced some now rare and correspondingly valuable figures. The exuberant pose of this porcelain girl, found with a variety of musical instruments and in different outfits, is typical. The hand-painted face is perhaps less expressive and appealing than faces by other manufacturers, but this shortcoming is more than offset by the long, sinous lines and vitality of the figure. Rarity and good condition explain the high value. The base is impressed with the model number; a written mark was used on later figures.

## ▼ "Butterfly girl" by Goldscheider

"Butterfly girl" is one of the most desirable Art Deco figures. She was made in three sizes (the largest is shown here), in a range of colours, with plain and patterned wings, and wearing either a hat or a head-dress. Her stylishness and dramatic pose, and the translucent quality of her wings, explain her appeal, and are typical of the fine figures by this Viennese firm (1885–1953). The base is marked underneath with the date, model number, and company stamp.

**FACT FILE**

- In general, German, Austrian, and Czech figures are more desirable than English designs because of their superior modelling and fine hand-painting.
- Most examples are highly stylized in boldly coloured, sometimes exotic, costumes.
- Figures in poses encapsulating the spirit of the "Jazz" age are extremely popular.
- Good condition is essential. Check carefully for restoration; tell-tale signs include subtle changes in skin tones and the glaze.

## ▼ Bathing girl by Rosenthal

The superb quality of porcelain by Rosenthal (est. 1879) was shown off to advantage in this classic Art Deco figure with delicate hand-painted flesh tones. The colour of the girl's hair is the same on all models, but she was made with either a matt or a high-gloss glaze. The blue of the towel is a colour often associated with Rosenthal; grey is also typical. Like all of the firm's figures, it is marked on the base with the company mark and an impressed model number.

"Butterfly girl", early 1930s, ht 41cm/16in, £2,500–3,500

Girl with a lyre, early 1930s, ht 27cm/10½in, £495–550

Bathing girl, late 1920s, ht 18cm/7in, £245–300

# Chintzware

In the 1920s and 1930s chintzware – tableware decorated with all-over floral patterns – was simply one of many affordable ranges manufactured for everyday use by such factories as Crown Ducal, Royal Winton (*see* pp.34-5), James Kent, Grimwades Ltd, and W.R. Midwinter. The pretty, fresh patterns were produced on transfer sheets and applied to an extensive range of shapes, with particular skill needed to cover irregular surfaces. Although quintessentially English, chintzware is now collected worldwide and has its own collecting clubs; budding collectors can refer to several detailed reference books for in-depth histories of the different patterns and information on production dates.

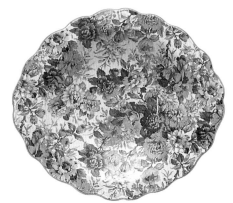

▼ **"Ivory Chintz" centrepiece by Crown Ducal**
Made by Crown Ducal (part of A.J. Richardson & Co. Ltd; est. 1915), this piece was intended to hold flowers and contains a ceramic "frog" – a pierced flower holder. A missing "frog" detracts greatly from the value, and one that is damaged is preferable to none at all. "Ivory Chintz", one of the earliest chintzware designs, features a bird hidden among the flowers. Slight crazing is acceptable, but scratching, fading, and restoration are not.

"Ivory Chintz" centrepiece, 1920s, diam. 25.5cm/10in, £195–225

▲ **"Peony" sweet dish by Crown Ducal**
The large size and attractive fluted edge of this piece make it very collectable, in spite of the scratch, which can be seen to the right of the centre. Although damage such as this will detract from the value, it is preferable to restoration in the form either of hand-painting or the use of another pattern. Any damage should be reflected in the price.

"Peony" sweet dish, late 1920s, diam. 18cm/7in, £95–125

"Du Barry" jam pot,
1930s, ht 9.5cm/3¾in,
£155–185

"Primrose" plate, 1930s,
diam. 23cm/9in, £95–115

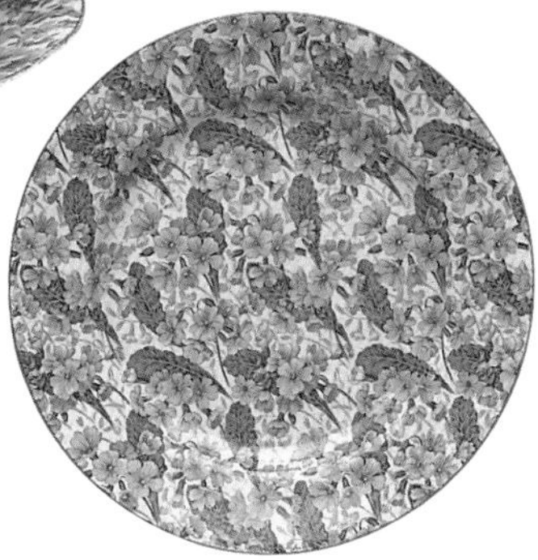

▲ "Du Barry" jam pot
by James Kent
The jam pot shown here is
an unusual shape and was
produced by this firm (est.
1897) for a limited period
only, because the base plate,
which is integral to the pot,
was so vulnerable. The best
examples are in perfect
condition, meaning that the
base plate and lid knob are
undamaged, and the pattern
is neither faded nor showing
any obvious joins; the pattern
should also match exactly
on the base and lid. The
differences between some
chintz patterns are difficult
to spot and should be checked
in one of the excellent
chintzware reference books.

▲ "Primrose" plate
by Crown Ducal
"Primrose" was usually
produced in yellow and
green, and the pink-and-green
version with an orange trim
shown here is so rare that this
piece may have been a sample.
Plates are particularly popular
with collectors as they can be
hung on a wall to show off the
pattern to its full advantage.

FACT FILE

• Chintzware is now a
highly popular collecting
area worldwide, and
prices reflect this. All
shapes are very desirable.
• The condition of the
transfer pattern is
crucial: clean-looking,
clear, crisp patterns
ensure maximum value;
fading, scratches, obvious
join lines, or inserts of
other patterns will all
detract from the value.
• Protruding features
such as spouts, lid
knobs, handles, and feet
need to be checked
carefully for damage.
• Avoid over-zealous
washing, use of abrasive
cleaning agents, and
exposure of chintzware
to bright sunlight, as all
three cause fading, which
is detrimental to value.

▼ "Springtime" biscuit
barrel by W.R. Midwinter
"Springtime" (also known as
"Brama"), which came with
either a green or a yellow trim,
is one of the most collectable
of the chintzware patterns by
Midwinter (est. 1910). This
biscuit barrel has the added
appeal of an unusual shape,
and hand-painted legs and
lid knob. Although attractive,
the legs and knob are very
susceptible to damage and
should be carefully checked
for chips, cracks, or
restoration. Although the
piece shown here has a
chrome handle, bamboo or
wicker handles are also found.

"Springtime" biscuit barrel,
late 1920s and 1930s, ht
(excluding handle) 13cm/5in,
£250–350

# Teaware

Teaware was produced in great quantity and variety in the 1920s and 1930s, when most familes had an earthenware tea-set for everyday use and a china set for "best". A complete set had six cups, saucers, and plates, plus a milk-jug, sugar-bowl, and cake plate (teapots and hot-water jugs were optional extras). However, complete sets are rare and highly priced, so most devotees collect cups and saucers, or "trios" – a matching cup, saucer, and plate – as self-contained collecting areas or with a view to building a full set. While major firms such as Shelley (*see* pp.36–9) made teaware for the top end of the market, many successful smaller factories such as W.H. Grindley & Co. and Adderleys Ltd made designs that are very desirable and more affordable.

◄ **"Royal Albert" trio by Thomas C. Wild & Sons**
The "Royal Albert" range made by the firm of Thomas C. Wild & Sons (est. 1917) included only a few fine Art Deco designs. Unusual features on this hand-painted trio include the pattern on the inside of the cup, the quirky angular handle, and the decorative moulding on the corners of the plate. Pieces produced after World War II combined transfer patterns with hand-painting and gilding. The trio bears a printed mark incorporating the company name, a crown, and the words "Crown China".

"Royal Albert" trio, 1930s, ht of cup 9cm/3½in, w. of plate 15cm/6in, £55–65

▼ **Trio by Adderleys**
The major appeal of this pretty china trio by the Staffordshire firm of Adderleys (est. 1906) lies in the innovative squared-off shape and the quality of the hand-painted floral pattern. The moulded floral handle – an extremely popular feature from c.1930 to the mid-1930s – is also a big attraction. Good condition is essential with china, as the smallest hairline crack will be easily visible and reduce the value.

Trio, 1930s, ht of cup 7cm/2¾in, w. of plate 15cm/6in, £65–85

This is one of many marks used by Grindley. Other designs feature a ship or a globe (or both).

## ▼ Trio by Grindley

The earthenware body of this trio suggests that it was made for everyday use in spite of the highly decorative floral handle. The robust body is complemented by the scale and vigour of the painted decoration. In addition to the multi-coloured version shown here, the firm (est. c.1880) also produced this design in single colours, including blue and pink.

Trio, 1930s, ht of cup 5cm/2in, diam. of plate 18cm/7in, **£65–85**

## ▼ Trio by Paragon

By the 1930s the Staffordshire firm of Paragon (est. c.1903) was one of the leading makers of china tableware with printed and enamelled decoration. The company's reputation was enhanced by royal patronage – much of its teaware, including the trio shown below, is stamped "Replica of service produced for Her Majesty Queen Mary". Paragon's nursery ware was also used by the princesses Elizabeth and Margaret Rose.

Trio, 1930s, ht of cup 7cm/2¾in, w. of plate 15cm/6in, **£65–85**

- In general, china is more sought after than earthenware.
- Pieces by well-known factories and in eye-catching shapes and patterns characteristic of the period are most popular; designs with moulded floral handles (typically Art Deco) are big favourites.
- Tea stains should never be removed with bleach or abrasive cleaners – try soaking stained pieces in denture cleaner instead.
- Always check handles and rims for hairline cracks, chips, or any sign of restoration.

## ▼ "Iris" trio by Royal Doulton

The "Iris" pattern shown here was also made in a blue-and-green colour scheme and with a very desirable solid flower-shaped handle; the solid handle was used from 1934 on the "luxury" model and is seen as more typically Art Deco than the more practical "open 7" handle shown here (used c.1931–8). In general tableware made after c.1938 by this firm (est. 1815) is less desirable than earlier wares.

"Iris" trio, 1930s, ht of cup 7cm/2¾in, diam. of plate 18cm/7in, **£65–85**

# Nursery ware

Although originally designed for children, nursery ware is now eagerly sought after by adult collectors. Wares from the 1930s featuring the newly created cartoon characters of the film-maker Walt Disney are probably most popular. Also highly sought after are designs commissioned by major firms from well-known children's book illustrators, for example Mabel Lucie Attwell's range commissioned by Shelley in the 1920s, and E.H. Shephard's "Christopher Robin" series, made from c.1927 for Ashstead's. The celebrated designers Clarice Cliff and Susie Cooper both worked on nursery ranges, as did the potters Charlotte Rhead (children's mugs for A.G. Richardson & Co., produced c.1934) and Barbara Vernon (a "Bunnykins" series for Royal Doulton based on Beatrix Potter's *Peter Rabbit* books).

Left to right: bear eggcup, 1930s, ht 6cm/2½in, **£25–30**; swan eggcup, 1930s, ht 6cm/2½in, **£17–25**

▲ **Animal eggcups**
Made of lustred earthenware, the designs shown above are typical of the eggcups (usually unmarked) that were mass-produced for export by German and Japanese makers. Novelty designs, which include rocking, whistling, and double eggcups, as well as those based on favourite cinema or cartoon characters, are very collectable. However, it is difficult to find examples in top condition as they were often treated roughly by children and damaged.

▼ **"Little Pig" toothbrush holder**
This violinist is one of a trio based on characters from the Disney cartoon *The Big Bad Wolf* and made for the British firm Maws & Co. (1850–c.1970). The other designs in the trio were a builder (in dungarees with a trowel) and a flautist; all three pigs were sold individually with a toothbrush (now rarely found with the mug). Other models include "Donald Duck", "Snow White and the Seven Dwarfs", and, most collectable, "Mickey Mouse" and "Minnie Mouse". Designs should be checked for chips and cracks on prominent details such as ears and hats.

"Little Pig" toothbrush holder, 1930s, ht 10cm/4in, **£85–95**

"Chicken" mug, 1932,
ht 9cm/3in, £185–200

Toothbrush mug, 1933,
ht 10cm/4in, £65–95

▲ **"Chicken" mug by Susie Cooper**
Cooper's nursery mugs were usually part of a porridge set also including a porringer and plate. The hand-painted design on the mug featured an animal – either a farmyard animal or one from the "Noah's Ark" range – and sometimes also a child's name. Although now highly sought after by collectors of nursery ware and Cooper fans alike, this nursery range was not a great success when first produced, as the hand-painted decoration seemed rather crude in comparison with the designer's other patterns (see pp.12–13). The range should be stamped with the "Susie Cooper Production" mark.

▲ **Toothbrush mug by Royal Cauldon**
The Staffordshire-based firm of Royal Cauldon (1774–1960s), which had a well-established reputation as a maker of quality wares, was granted a royal warrant in 1924. This child's toothbrush mug was part of an earthenware jug-and-basin set decorated with charming transfer-printed and hand-painted designs of nursery rhymes, in this case *Ride a Cock Horse to Banbury Cross*. Other nursery rhymes in this series include *Mary Had a Little Lamb* and *Baa Baa Black Sheep*.

**FACT FILE**

• Although major designers produced ranges, charm and appeal may override a well-known name.
• Wares showing Disney characters and well-known characters from children's literature are extremely popular.
• Smaller pieces such as eggcups are a good starting-point for new collectors, as they can be modestly priced.
• Condition is crucial; the rough and tumble of life in the nursery has meant that few pieces have survived unscathed.

▼ **Chamber pot by Shelley**
The highly collectable nursery-ware range commissioned from Attwell by Shelley (see pp.36–9) included cups and saucers, mugs, plates, teapots, napkin rings, and, most sought after, figures. All designs in the range, except for the chamber pots and napkin rings, featured a verse of two or more lines. Chamber pots, which were also made in an even smaller size than this example, were decorated with two, three, or four transfer-printed images (always including a pixie) with a hand-painted trim; Attwell's printed signature appears on the front of the bowl.

Chamber pot, c.1930s,
ht 9cm/3in, £350–400

# Face masks

African art was highly influential in the evolution of the exotic Art Deco style, and the ceramic face masks now so closely connected with the period were probably inspired by imported African wooden face masks, which were eagerly collected at that time. Ceramic masks, typically modelled on such famous film stars as Dorothy Lamour and Marlene Dietrich, or on highly fashionable young women, were produced in profile, face on, and in sets by a wide variety of factories in Europe. Bold colours and sharp contours are typical. Important manufacturers in Britain include J.H. Cope & Co. Ltd and John Beswick Ltd, both in Staffordshire. Austrian makers, notably Royal Dux, Friedrich Goldscheider, and Goebels, are also renowned for their striking, top-quality designs.

▼ **Woman in profile by Cope**

This mask features an archetypal smart, sophisticated, and fashionable Art Deco woman. It was made as a blonde, a red-head, and a brunette, with or without a hat of various colours. All face masks by Cope (1887–c.1945) have a high-gloss glaze; most show the left profile, although some are face on and a few feature the right profile. Cope masks are extremely desirable, so watch out for copies; the latter can often be distinguished from the originals by the lack of the impressed "C. & Co." mark on the back.

Woman in profile, 1930s, l. 15cm/6in, £95–125

▼ **"Marlene" by Beswick**

Dietrich's distinctive features – her arched eyebrows and almond-shaped eyes – made her a favourite subject for face masks. This example is the most popular of the "Marlene" masks by Beswick (est. 1840), although it was also made with Dietrich's trademark platinum-blonde hair, with a green or a blue beret, and (less common) in profile. Early models have a high-gloss glaze; post-war models have a matt glaze. All examples have a model number on the back.

"Marlene", 1934, l. 24cm/9in, £275–295

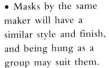

## "Dorothy Lamour" by Goebels

Superb modelling and hand-painting combined with rarity make face masks by Goebels particularly popular with collectors. The firm produced both face-on masks and, less common, designs in profile, as well as a very collectable range of double-face masks, with two faces in profile looking at one other. "Dorothy Lamour" was hand-painted with a satin glaze and made in several sizes. It should be checked carefully for damage to the plaits and roses. All examples bear an impressed company mark and a model number.

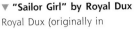

## "Sailor Girl" by Royal Dux

Royal Dux (originally in Vienna, later in Czechoslovakia – now the Czech Republic) is particularly renowned for its fine figures and face masks (including some examples based on men). "Sailor Girl" featured below, which was produced in matt, satin, and high-gloss glazes and as a blonde, brunette, and red-head, was one of a range based on the armed services.

"Sailor Girl", 1930, l. 17cm/6¾in, **£200–245**

- Masks by the same maker will have a similar style and finish, and being hung as a group may suit them.
- A dirty mask can be cleaned with warm soapy water and a sponge or soft toothbrush. With stubborn dirt, allow the mask to soak. Never use bleaches or abrasives.
- Copies of Goldscheider masks, which are difficult to differentiate from the originals, are made in Europe today. The safest guarantee of authenticity is to buy from a reputable dealer.

## Terracotta red-head by Goldscheider

The quality of the modelling on masks by Goldscheider (1885–1953) puts them into the top collecting bracket. They were made of hand-painted terracotta, usually with stylized, often pierced eyes and a satin glaze. Terracotta is soft and damages easily, so check the condition. If unobtrusive, minor chips are acceptable, but avoid examples that have been restored. This mask has the characteristic elaborately moulded curly hair, which although well modelled, has two small chips, which are reflected in the price.

"Dorothy Lamour", late 1920s/early 1930s, l. 18cm/7in, **£175–200**

Terracotta red-head, 1930s, l. 31cm/12in, **£750–950**

# Novelty ware

Most British factories produced earthenware novelties as cheerful, inexpensive money-spinners during the economic gloom of the 1920s and 1930s. Designers came up with whimsical and ingenious designs to brighten up everyday tableware such as jugs, cruet sets, jam pots, honey pots, and napkin rings, as well as such purely decorative items as hand-bells. There is a huge range to choose from, with prices to match most budgets. Many collectors have a favourite theme based on either the design (bears, bees, or cartoon characters, for example), the size (miniatures are very popular), or the form (most notably sugar-shakers and cruet sets).

▼ **"Pixie" jug by Royal Winton**
The penchant for fairies and pixies in the 1920s and 1930s was endorsed by Queen Mary and promoted by various factories. Royal Winton brought out a now rare and valuable "Pixie" series of moulded and hand-painted designs such as sugar-shakers, teapots, vases, jam pots, sweet baskets, and the jug shown here. This piece was produced in two sizes, with the pixie in different colours including pink, green, mauve, and yellow. Restoration is not acceptable on this range, so check for flaking paint and wear on the handle.

"Pixie" jug, 1936, ht 23cm/9in, **£195–225**

▼ **"Butterfly" dish by John Beswick Ltd**
Although the butterfly is a popular decorative motif, butterfly shapes such as this hand-painted dish designed to hold jam and butter are rare. This piece was made in various sizes and colours, all with impressed model numbers and a painter's mark. Beswick (est. 1840) is a top factory, and such a dish will appeal to both collectors of insect novelties and Beswick fans, provided that there are no chips or cracks, or any flaking paint.

"Butterfly" dish, 1930, w. 17cm/6¾in, **£35–45**

"Apple" jam pot, late 1920s,
ht 9cm/3in, £45–55

Coronet Ware sugar-shaker,
1930s, ht 15cm/6in, £45–55

### ▲ "Apple" jam pot by Mintons

As well as the rare and collectable "apple" jam pot featured above, the Staffordshire firm of Mintons (est. 1793) also manufactured versions of this jam pot in the form of "oranges" and "grapes". This piece features the high-quality hand-painting typical of the firm, but the "stalk" handle is easy to damage and should be checked carefully for chips, cracks, or restoration. The printed mark of the factory appears on the base.

### ▲ Coronet Ware sugar-shaker by Parrott & Co.

Sugar-shakers are very popular with collectors and come in a huge variety of patterns and shapes. This moulded example in an unusual footed shape with hand-painted decoration is from the Coronet Ware range made by the Staffordshire firm of Parrott (est. c.1921). Good condition is essential. The top must be present – the one shown here is chrome, but silver plate was also used – and it should be removable, so that the rim can be checked for damage or restoration, which will affect the value.

## FACT FILE

- Novelties are a good starting-point for new collectors, as charm, humour, and unusual shape and design are in general more important than a big name.
- Many factories brought out novelty ranges in the 1920s and 1930s, so the choice is very wide.
- Condition is important as most pieces are very affordable. Pay special attention to vulnerable areas, which chip easily.
- Look for pieces that span different collecting areas, such as a piece with an animal theme by a well-known factory.

Carlton Ware hand-bell, 1930s, ht 10cm/4in, £95–125

### ◀ Carlton Ware hand-bell by Wiltshaw & Robinson

This bell, known as "Toff", is one of a rare series, which also includes "French Maid", "Bell Boy", and "Ring Master". Each bell should be complete with its ceramic clanger, which should be attached by a wire. A missing clanger (or an inappropriate replacement), cracks, or repainting will all detract from the value. This bell has a small chip on the hat, which is reflected in a reduced price.

**MARKS**

This mark was used by Mintons from c.1912. A mark with the globe, or globe and crown only, signifies an earlier piece.

"Honeycomb" box by Crown Devon, 1930s, ht 10cm/4in, **£95–115**

Double jam pot, 1930s, ht 10cm/4in, **£50–60** (single **£30–40**)

Pin-cushion doll, 1930s, ht 15cm/6in, **£65–85**

### ▲ Double jam pot

The Staffordshire firm of Arthur Wood & Son Ltd (est. 1884) produced a variety of inexpensive ranges, many of which borrowed heavily from other factories' designs. The hand-painted double jam pot shown here was also made as a single version and in several colour schemes, with either a silver or a gold trim. The example in pastel colours shown here was not especially popular and was produced only for a short period. A double jam pot is more collectable than a single pot, provided that both lids are present and the silver or gold trim is not badly rubbed. This piece has the transfer-printed company backstamp and the painter's mark.

### ▲ Crown Devon "honeycomb" box

Designs with a bee theme, particularly honey pots, are perennially popular with collectors. The "honeycomb" box shown is unusual, and rarity adds to the value. The body is moulded to create a "honeycomb" texture and decorated with several hand-painted "bees". The free-standing "bee" with wide-spread wings on the top indicates that this piece is one of the earlier, more collectable versions. The "bee" was vulnerable and in the late 1930s was moulded into the box and given closed wings. Earlier versions should be carefully checked for damage to the "bee's" wings and legs.

### ▲ Pin-cushion doll

These dolls form another self-contained and highly popular novelty collecting niche. Examples, many of which were made in Germany, were manufactured in a variety of heights and styles but usually have an impressed number below the waist. The example shown here has the characteristic moulded ceramic upper body and legs with hand-painted details. Designs in which the arms were outstretched are rarely found as they were so easily damaged, and any details in high relief should be carefully checked for restoration. Moulded upper bodies were also used as handles for powder puffs, powder bowls, and brushes.

- Good condition is essential for novelty ware. Very minor damage is acceptable on an extremely rare piece, but it must be reflected in the price. Check any protruding areas very carefully for damage.
- There is a wide range of prices, beginning with such modestly priced pieces as eggcups and moving up to "Toby" or character jugs by Royal Doulton.
- Musical novelties, if still in good working order, are very desirable.
- Disney characters are at a premium, as are characters from well-known children's books such as *Winnie-the-Pooh* and Beatrix Potter's *Peter Rabbit* series. Film characters and animal designs are also popular.

### ▼ "Cat" pot

The popularity of the cat pictures by Louis Wain inspired a whole range of cat pots, ranging from models by Clarice Cliff (see pp.8–11) to the quirky design shown here. Made in Czechoslovakia (now the Czech Republic) in a variety of hand-painted colours, it was one of several whimsical animal wares including dogs, ducks, and frogs. On this example the head lifts off, so that the body can be used as a pot, but this design was also made as a jug. With such modestly priced pieces restoration is unacceptable; ears, in particular, should be checked carefully for chips or cracks.

### ▼ "Laurel and Hardy" salt and pepper pots

The film success enjoyed by Stan Laurel and Oliver Hardy sparked the design of many novelty wares in their image. This ingenious design by Beswick (est. 1840) includes a separate base with indentations in which their heads sit side by side. The moulded heads were hand-painted in a variety of flesh tones; deeper tones are more desirable than paler versions. The complete set is rare (the base is often missing), but the salt and pepper pots can be collected separately and put together as a set. As individual pieces, "Hardy" is more popular than "Laurel".

"Cat" pot, c.1930s, ht 15cm/6in, **£45–65**

"Laurel and Hardy" salt and pepper pots, 1934, ht 10cm/4in, **£75–95** (£50–60 without base)

# Glossary

**Art Deco** style, fashionable from c.1918 to 1940, typified by geometric designs and bold, bright colours; the name was inspired by the title of the Exhibition of Decorative and Modern Industrial Arts, held in 1925 in Paris

**backstamp** identification mark used on the underside of a piece; usually made with a rubber stamp, but can also refer to mark made by incising, impressing, hand-painting, or printing

**basalt** name used by Wedgwood for a range of unglazed black stoneware

**biscuit** unglazed china or earthenware that has been fired once

**"bloom"** term used to describe the discoloration of dark blue and black lead-based paints exposed to direct sunlight, harsh detergents, or over-zealous washing

**body** main part of a piece, as opposed to the handle, spout, lid etc; also refers to the clay from which a piece is made

**bone china** type of porcelain modified by the addition of bone ash

**celadon** a semi-translucent glaze, usually pale green or green-grey

**charger** large plate or platter

**china** term commonly used for porcelain and bone china

**chinoiserie** type of European pseudo-Chinese decoration featuring figures, pagodas, dragons, birds etc

**chintzware** designs decorated with all-over floral transfer-printed patterns

**coffee-can** cylindrical, straight-sided cup

**commemorative wares** pieces made to commemorate a historical event (eg a battle, coronation, or exhibition)

**cottage ware** ornaments in the shape of cottages

**crazing** tiny cracks in the surface of the glaze

**earthenware** pottery that does not vitrify when fired and is porous if not glazed

**enamelling** decoration in enamels

**enamels** colours derived from metallic oxides and applied as overglaze decoration

**engine-turned** type of incised decoration produced by turning unfired pottery on a machine-driven lathe

**flatware** flat or shallow tableware such as plates

**"frog"** pierced shape that fits into a vase to hold flowers

**glaze** glassy coating that gives a smooth, sometimes shiny, finish and is used to seal porous bodies

**ground** background area onto which decoration is added

**impressed mark** indented (as opposed to incised) mark

**incised** scratched into the surface with a sharp point

**in-glaze** decoration sandwiched between two layers of glaze

**lustre** a metallic, sometimes iridescent, type of glaze

**moulded** form produced by pressing clay into a mould

**on-glaze** decoration applied after the piece has been glazed

**overglaze** painted or printed decoration applied after glazing

**porcelain** translucent white ceramic ware fired at a high temperature

**pottery** general term for all ceramic wares except porcelain

**slip** creamy mixture of clay and water used for decoration

**stamped** term used to describe a piece marked with a rubber stamp prior to firing

**stoneware** type of ceramic body that has a firing temperature midway between earthenware and porcelain

**terracotta** lightly fired, red-toned earthenware

**thrown** pieces shaped by hand on a rotating wheel

**transfer-printed** type of decoration where the design is transferred from an inked engraving to paper and from paper to the ceramic shape

**tube-lining** type of decoration in which the slip is "piped" onto the body to create raised lines

**underglaze** designs applied before glazing

# Where to buy

New collectors are advised to buy from established auction houses, reputable dealers (members of the antiques associations LAPADA and BADA), and vetted fairs such as trade fairs and events organized by collectors' clubs.

## MAJOR AUCTION HOUSES

**Bonhams (Chelsea)**
65–9 Lots Road
London SW10 0RN

**Christie's**
8 King Street
St James's
London SW1Y 6QT

**Christie's South Kensington**
85 Old Brompton Road
London SW7 3LD

**Phillips**
101 New Bond Street
London W1Y 0AS

**Sotheby's**
34–35 New Bond Street
London W1A 2AA

## ART DECO DEALERS

**Beth Adams**
Alfies Antique Market
13–25 Church Street
Marylebone
London NW8 8DT

**Beverley Adams**
30 Church Street
Marylebone
London NW8 8EP

**Bizarre Decorative Arts**
116 Manchester Road
Altrincham WA14 4PY

**Muir Hewitt**
Halifax Antiques Centre
Queens Road Mills
Queens Road/Giblet Street
Halifax HX1 4LN

**Tango**
22 Kenilworth Road
Knowle
Solihull B93 0JA

## ANTIQUES MARKETS

**Alfies Antique Market**
13–25 Church Street
Marylebone
London NW8 8DT

**Antiquarius Antiques Market**
131–141 King's Road
London SW3 8DT

**Camden Passage Antique Centre**
12 Camden Passage
Islington
London N1 8ED

**Grays Antique Market**
58 Davies Street
London W1Y 1LL

## COLLECTORS' CLUBS

**The Beswick Collectors' Circle**
Corner Cottage
Hedgerley Lane
Gerrards Cross SL9 7NS

**Carlton Ware Collectors International**
PO Box 161
Sevenoaks
Kent TN15 6GA

**Clarice Cliff Collectors' Club**
Fantasque House
Tennis Drive
The Park
Nottingham NG7 1AE

**Susie Cooper Collectors' Group**
PO Box 48
Beeston
Nottingham NG9 2RN

**Royal Doulton International Collectors' Society**
Minton House
London Road
Stoke-on-Trent ST4 7QD

**Torquay Pottery Collectors' Society**
Avenue Road
Torre Abbey
Torquay TQ2 5JX

# What to read

There are many excellent books on ceramics of this period, and the following is just a small selection. This list includes both general books and titles on specific designers and factories, all of which should be available either from good bookshops and libraries, or through collectors' clubs.

**GENERAL**

**Arwas, V.** *Art Deco* (London, 1992)

**Buckley, C.** *Potters and Paintresses: Women Designers in the Pottery Industry 1870–1955* (London, 1990)

**Spours, J.** *Art Deco Tableware* (London, 1988)

**Watson, H. and P.** *Collecting Art Deco Ceramics* (London, 1993)

**INDIVIDUAL DESIGNERS AND FACTORIES**

**Atterbury, P.** *Moorcroft Pottery: A Guide to the Pottery of William and Walter Moorcroft, 1897–1986* (London, 1987)

**Batkin, M.** *Wedgwood Ceramics, 1846–1959: A New Appraisal* (London, 1982)

**Bumpus, B.** *Charlotte Rhead, Potter & Designer* (London, 1987)

**Casey, A.** *Susie Cooper Ceramics: A Collector's Guide* (Stratford-on-Avon, 1992)

**Eberle, L. and Scott, S.** *The Carlton Standard Catalogue of Chintz* (London, 1997)

**Eyles, D., Irvine, L., and Baynton, V.** *Royal Doulton Figures* (Shepton Beauchamp, 1994)

**Hawkins, J.** *The Poole Potteries* (London, 1980)

**Hill, S.** *Crown Devon* (Stratford-on-Avon, 1996)

**Hill, S.** *The Shelley Style: A Collector's Guide* (Stratford-on-Avon, 1990)

**Irvine, L.** *Royal Doulton "Bunnykins" Collector's Book* (Shepton Beauchamp, 1993)

**Joseph, F.** *Collecting Carlton Ware* (London, 1994)

**Miller, M.** *Collecting Royal Winton* (London, 1994)

**Miller, M.** *The Royal Winton Collectors Handbook* (London, 1998)

**Niblett, K.** *Hand-painted Gray's Pottery* (Stoke-on-Trent, 1982)

**Torquay Pottery Collectors' Society** *Torquay Motto Wares* (Torquay, 1989)

**Watson, H. and P.** *Collecting Clarice Cliff* (London, 1995)

# Index

**Acknowledgments**
All pictures copyright Octopus Publishing Group Ltd. All pictures photographed by Tim Ridley,
courtesy of Beverley Adams and Beth Adams except:
**19l** Octopus Publishing Group Ltd/Chris Halton; **17c, 18l, 18c, 18r, 32l, 32r, 33bl, 33t** Octopus
Publishing Group Ltd/Miller's, Kent; **19r** Octopus Publishing Group Ltd/Premier Photography; **2** Octopus
Publishing Group Ltd/Steve Tanner. **Jacket photograph** Octopus Publishing Group Ltd/Steve Tanner.